Why I Love Running

Chasing Dreams and Breaking Barriers: The Power of Running in My Life

ISBN 978-0-9869317-8-9

Published in USA, Canada, Mexico and Kenya

© 2024 by Nelson Ndereva

Preface

In this narrative of "Why I Love Running," Nelson Ndereva takes us on an intimate journey through his life, woven intricately with the rhythm of his footsteps on the pavement. As a seasoned runner with a passion for the sport, Ndereva invites readers to lace up their shoes and join him as he navigates the ups and downs of his extraordinary running career. From the bustling streets of Nairobi to the tranquil paths of Mount Kenya, each step is imbued with the essence of his unwavering dedication and love for the sport.

This captivating narrative not only chronicles Ndereva's personal experiences but also delves into the broader cultural significance of running in Kenya. As he shares anecdotes from his training camps and races, readers gain insight into the unique blend of talent, discipline, and camaraderie that defines the Kenyan running community. Through the author's eyes, we come to understand why running is not merely a physical activity but a way of life deeply rooted in Kenyan culture.

But "Why I Love Running" is more than just a memoir; it's a testament to the transformative power of the sport. Ndereva reveals how running has shaped his character, instilling in him qualities of perseverance, resilience, and humility. With every mile, he discovers new depths of self-awareness and finds solace in the rhythmic pounding of his feet against the earth.

In this stirring tribute to the sports he holds dear, Ndereva invites readers to embrace the joy of running, reminding us that every step forward is a testament to the indomitable spirit of the human heart. Through his words, we are inspired to chase our dreams, conquer our fears, and discover the boundless potential that lies within us all.

***

Dedication

To JL Seymore,

 for your unwavering support and love
throughout my career. Your motivation and
guidance, seen through the lenses of an athlete,
have been invaluable. You believed in me when
others doubted, and your faith kept me going
even in the toughest times. Thank you for being
my mentor, my friend, and my greatest
supporter.

— Nelson Ndereva

To my family in Kenya,

for their utmost display of love and their innermost affection that sustained me through every challenge. Your encouragement and sacrifices have been the bedrock of my journey. Without your support, I would not have achieved my dreams. I am forever grateful for your endless love and belief in me.

— Nelson Ndereva

To my beloved brother,

who steadfastly followed the painful path of my sports endeavors. Your dedication and loyalty have been a source of strength for me. You have shared my struggles; my triumphs and your presence has made the journey more meaningful. Thank you for walking this path with me.

— Nelson Ndereva

And to all my sports fans,

 who celebrated with me along the way. Your cheers, your support, and your belief in my abilities have fueled my passion and drive. I love you all and thank you for being with me throughout this incredible journey.

— Nelson Ndereva

In this book

1. The challenges and adversities faced by athletes in Kenya's athletics scene, including mismanagement of funds and logistical issues.
2. The camaraderie and solidarity among athletes during difficult times, highlighting the importance of teamwork and support.
3. Insights into the bureaucratic hurdles and shortcomings within sports administration, particularly in the context of organizing athletic events.
4. The perseverance and resilience exhibited by athletes in the face of setbacks and disappointments.

5. The impact of financial constraints on athletes' experiences, from transportation woes to basic necessities like food and accommodation.
6. The role of community support and solidarity in overcoming obstacles, as seen in the athletes' collective efforts to raise funds for transportation.
7. The determination and passion driving athletes to pursue their dreams despite systemic challenges and institutional shortcomings.
8. The complexities of balancing athletic aspirations with practical considerations such as funding and logistical support.
9. The valuable lessons learned from adversity, including the importance of adaptability, resourcefulness, and unity.

***

Why I Love Running

Chasing Dreams and Breaking Barriers: The Power of Running in My Life

My passion for sports and physical agility blossomed at a remarkably early age. I had great appetite for sports engagements; occasionally finding myself in various stunts where I played any game that came my way. While I lacked the physical and muscular strength required for contact sports such as Soccer, Judo, Snatch-Ball, Volleyball and Rugby, which were introduced in school, I navigated these limitations with grace. Some of these sports posed their own set of challenges due to my stature, yet my enthusiasm for sports continued to drive me to explore and excel in various athletic pursuits.

Running was of course a milestone toward transforming me where I gained better understanding of myself, my body and its purpose in life through actively engaging in sports. But how I ended up being a runner is an enthralling sportsmanship manifestation at a very early age.

The unexpected turn of events occurred one day at school when the games teacher blew the whistle prompting every student to hurriedly exit the classroom and assemble on the circle where we paraded every morning before class and on Fridays which was National Flag Day. It was the third week of the second term of my midgrade class. Unaware of the proceedings, I found myself caught up in the mixed commotion; in my mind the assumption was that the parading was called for us to go home. I rushed to the classroom to pick up my books. I soon noticed that it's not a call to go home because no one had their books, a student whispered to me that its games time. I hurriedly took my books back to the classroom. This confusion made me miss the instructions by the game's teacher; by the time I reached at the parading area the entire school was collectively running towards a destination unfamiliar to me. Confused, I hesitated to run too far ahead, uncertain of the route they were taking as it deviated from the path I knew going home. Later, I discovered that Tuesday and Thursday afternoons were designated as school games days which required all students' participation. It was cross country season and we engaged in this running practice to select a team for our school. The selected school team would progress through division, district, and provincial levels, ultimately aiming for the National championship held at the president's home.

In my inaugural cross-country run. I returned to school without knowing what was all this about. I was among those who were left way behind; the teacher waited with a cane at the school entrance, chasing us while caning whoever he caught up with in the final stretch.

I was eager to find out who was the top runner in the school. To my amazement it was none other than my immediate neighbor, Stephen Mucimbi. Intrigued by his achievement I felt a strong desire to engage with him, not knowing precisely what to ask but simply yearning to be his close friend. Stephen, a remarkably reserved individual maintained a quiet demeanor in school and at home. Despite his reserved nature, he was a highly accomplished student, earning the title of the cleanest student of the year for numerous consecutive years. Furthermore, he garnered several prestigious running awards, establishing himself as an exceptional athlete. Unlike other children, Stephen refrained from engaging in typical playful activities; instead, he remained composed and silent. The same year I saw my first track and field events which I learned their names while trying any that come across. High jump, Pole vault and running were my fascinations. My love for Pole Vault was such an amusement; I would later get wild simulating the game, jumping corn rows in our farm; sometimes crushing on series of rows attracting stern warning from my mother. Incidentally at one time while Pole-vaulting at our corn farm, I lodged an ankle dislocation which made my mother carry me on her back to the hospital. Advertently after recovery I received a beating from my stunts bringing my love for Pole-vault to an end.

I watch Stephens sensational performances as he scored collectively all middle-distance events on the track. His prowess extended to dominating the field in the eight hundred meters, fifteen hundred meters and cross-country events throughout the entire province. That year I watch Stephen compete in all levels until he was eliminated at the provincials after finishing third in contested repeats. He had finished in second position twice at the finals with judges contesting the results; they were determined to eliminate him in technical grounds discriminatively as they just needed two top finishers and he wasn't their favored candidate.

Stephen become my role model and I envied his running achievements, unfortunately I never ran again with Stephen as he graduated the same year after this remarkable incident. Due to illness Stephen never continued with running after elementary school.

With the exit of Stephen and his class from the school, a new dawn opened for younger generations to showcase their talents; from that time my presence in school competitions was more pronounced, I dreaded to be just like Stephen.

It was quite easy for me lapping other students in various events which involved a couple of laps. Men's or women's turns, it didn't matter to me; I embraced each race as a thrilling experience; reveling in the sheer fun of being part of it. I played unwarranted mischief during the school's track and field events. While any group of runners lined up to start their event. I would position myself at the corner of the track waiting for them then as they draw closer to me, I will hop in, run with them and drop before the last stretch of the final lap. This went on for several instances until sports teacher took it very seriously and in turn, I would be punished for entering events without permission. It didn't take long for me to recognize a natural gift within me, an innate talent for running that set me apart in the world of sports.

Throughout my early school years, I enthusiastically embraced participation in all school activities. In particular, during the running season, I consistently made myself available and eager to represent my school. In those years, the emphasis wasn't solely on how fast one could run but also on physical appearance. Unfortunately, some students, despite their athletic abilities, were reluctant to participate in school sports for unknown reasons. It was normal for teachers to head pick students with more robust physiques over individuals who may appear petite or shorter by statue even if they possessed equal or greater running abilities leading to a biased selection process.

Extracurricular activities included Drama and Art, propelling us towards schools' provincial competitions. I was the worst in Art and Craft mainly because I could never find raw materials as needed. I remember getting punished on every art class for lack of any art project. Some involved going to the forest and finding ideal wood for any item proposed to you by your teacher.

***

Growing up in Africa is indeed one way of developing natural resistance on anything other than sickness. Whenever I compared the situation in my family and the situation with our neighbors, there was obvious contrast that somehow left blanks in my young mind; we had no food, no clothing, we never harvested anything from our farm despite hard work, we would consume everything before its maturity. My mother became heartbroken and desperate.

As an elder son and upon exposure to this dreaded life I became hopeless and helpless too. Although my dad was a civil servant, he was unable to cover all our upkeep and essential without mentioning education. Our living quarters were filthy and numerous days we slept hungry. Before moving to my own living space, I had witnessed shocking deplorable state of our only house. The roof had visible tiny holes that the moonlight would shine through at night. The same hole would be the reason our beds would soak from drops on water during rainy days.

This constant leaking roof made the mud walls weak causing parts of the walls to fall off now and then. After every rainy season we would in turn re-surface the walls with fresh mud paste. Failure to do this in time the walls would develop crack and tiny mud elements would fall off which happened a few times; consequently, one could see what was happening outside from your bed. Insects would also find pathways into your bed; rats would hide on those cracking walls and creep through your bed across to the kitchen looking for food leftovers. It was normal ones in while finding a toad hiding behind stationary items. Snakes were none exceptional, the presence of rats attracted snakes too often found within the cracked walls

On the other hand, for us to be sent home from school for lack of tuition was an inescapable exercise which was well executed by the head of the school. It became normal that our parents were among the parents defaulting to pay school fees which had annual increment. We never missed in the headmaster's shortlist to be sent home.

Annoyingly, my sibling and I would never stick in school for longer than a month without a break. One week we would be sent home for school fees, the next week another kid would be sent for torn school uniform, the other week for textbooks and not mentioning other simple things like pens, during that time students were not allowed to use ballpoints which our dad brought in abundance, we had to use ink pens what were fragile and delicate to maintain. Our mother became a working horse to cater for our never ending school needs.

It was embarrassing to witness oneself walking home during class times; once sent home for lack of any of the school essentials, the cunning villagers who were aware of our family poverties would tease us mockingly commenting the shorter school hours; they would ask us where are schoolmates from the community.

To overcome these stressful comings, we dwelt in a very laborious culture; working at our neighbors' farms for food, clothing and for every necessity in life. Often my mother would at times instruct me to meet her in the forest after school always after our class time. I would go straight to the forest where I met her laboring for either cash or food as a pay. Crossing the forest on my own at a young age was never easy but I always built my fearlessness and curiosity.

It was during those times that I learned various skills of survival although the hard way. I mean the hard way because I will get teased and attacked by mature kids as I grew up until I build my own defense mechanism.

***

By the age of twelve, I found life full of sentimental scenes unfolding, witnessing my younger sister soothing a crying sibling with a lullaby while our mother is late at neighbor's farm toiling for our food. As the dusk settled and as we waited our mother would return with sustenance for her starving children. The child's persistent cries revealed the harsh reality of hunger. This particular day and its recurring memory haunted me at the time triggering a flow of tears. I recall the natural sisterly love my younger sister exhibited, assuming the role of a nurturing mother as she sang to the baby, patiently awaiting our mother's return from her demanding work.

The complexity of our lives unfolded gradually, with our mother shouldering the family's burdens alone. At times during our forest excursions, I played the role of babysitter for my siblings while my mother would toil in farms in the forest. We lived by courage and fearlessness of the unknown predicaments of nature.

After completing my elementary school, I gained admission to Mbiruri High School Embu in Kenya, approximately twenty kilometers away from home.

In anticipation of entering high school, the moment arrived for my transformation from a boy to a man. I ventured to meet the notorious man-maker; a stern figure known for intentionally breaking down the boyish spirit to instill valuable lessons. He was a stack build and ready to wrestle lads in case they attempt to run midway as he performed his craftiness. Lined up in the ritual were some anxious classmates who shared ominous tales about the craftsman's disdain for young boys, warning that he would deliberately challenge and push us beyond our limits.

On the day of the inevitable boy-to-man event, amidst the palpable fear, I watched some boys nervously shifted positions moving back to the end of the line unsure of what awaited them for fear especially if the boy in active operation screamed or walked out crying. When my turn came, I approached the craftsman with a determination for courage to endure whatever lay ahead. The experience unfolded as one of the most profound in my entire life. After the ordeal, I walked to where my counselor awaited, who didn't believe the art was performed that fast; so he quickly inquired if the craftsman had taken a tea break or if something was wrong, maybe he thought I was and escapee. I stoically replied in the negative, concealing the pain within me. Determined to proceed, I declared my readiness, and my counselor handed me ten shillings for transportation. We headed to the bus stage, and he instructed one of his workers who had come to get flour from the mill, "Go with Nelson; he is not feeling well," and promptly departed.

After a few minutes, the man inquired about my choice to wait for public transportation, suggesting that the money intended for transportation could be better used elsewhere; given that we are poor and we are within a walking distance from home. He proposed an alternative; with a bag of corn flour in his possession, he suggested taking turns carrying the bag to hasten our journey home. The proposition hung in the air, prompting me to weigh the options and make a decision.

Unbeknownst to him, I had just been undergone a significant rite of passage leaving behind a part of me to the craftsman. In response, I conveyed a positive affirmation, concealing any indication of the discomfort I was experiencing. As we traversed three kilometers, we took turns carrying the fifteen-kilogram bag of corn flour, moving forward with a regal demeanor, steadfast and silent amidst the concealed pain of my recently acquired secret burdens. As I bore the double-edged suffering of carrying the bag of corn flour while concealing my pain, the bandage between my legs became soaked with blood, increasing my fear of staining my pants. I didn't know if it was wise to reveal to my comrade about my missing portion, so I remained silent. I also imagined myself collapsing midway and being exposed.

We arrived near our home and said goodbye to the worker and walked to home to nurse myself as I was bleeding and in pain. My mother was delighted and asked me if I was treated further indicating she didn't notice any vehicle stop by the entrance which was our normal drop off for anyone destined to our home. She didn't expect me with to be walking steady with intentionally planned wounds. Maybe she also thought I have joined the class of the one notorious man in the community who is said to have escaped the craftsman wrath and disappeared for years without returning home. When he returned home no one would dare ask him if he underwent the cut because he was fully grown and wore a turban, a religious sect attire that carried a statue of trust. In response to my mother, I said "yes, the treatment was done and we didn't wait for transportation but we walked home". My mother smiled as I proceeded to climb up my dungeon.

During the time I sleeping den was an typical African food storage unit. It was built on a platform raised four feet high leveled for the purposed of keeping food dry; its walls were made of thin wood threaded together and inter-twined to make a wooden mesh to allow fresh air to keep the produce fresh. It was common for young boys to reside on these amazing structures, there was no conventional bed. My sleeping arrangement was makeshift bed made from dried banana leaves stashed on a sack to make a comfortable mattress. Making the bed required thorough observation scanning for crawling insect or spiders from these dried banana leaves. Residing in this food storage platform was fun, providing me with a view of the entire compound and appeared as safe sentry when there was moonlight.

***

Whispers of my initiation circulated rapidly throughout the village. My mother knew about the unethical practices in accordance with tradition and was ready to protect her son from this brutality. The newly initiated young men were expected to fulfill certain requirements; extortion and demands were imposed to the newly initiated.

These practices were transferred from one generation to the other which acted as the previous group that had gone through similar rituals as a payback. This ritual involved offering gratuities to your seniors, and for those who smoked, providing a stash of cigarettes in your room. Some demanded a gallon of traditional beer, while others had peculiar and inexplicable requests.

Failure to meet these demands often resulted in torment, especially during the most sensitive period of one's recovery from the crafty ritual. The initiation process could involve various forms of mistreatment, including handling one's manhood, leading to discomfort and even bleeding. In some instances, initiates were paraded outside, compelled to undertake peculiar tasks, or subjected to mockery by age-mate girls alongside their fellow tormentors. In my situation, I found protection under my counselor, who held a position of authority in the community for providing jobs for young men in his company that delt with forest products; cutting wood to supply firewood to schools, hospital and other institutions, and clearing forest. Perhaps even significantly it was the fact that I could not host any guest as I resided in a structure that required climbing up few flights of wooden steps.

It was a long joyous moment for a young teen transitioning moment before proceeding with further education.

Due to financial constraints, my parents were not able support my education for the whole four years leading me to engage in home schooling. Acquainted with studying at home from an early age didn't stop me from facing more challenges along the way. In between studies, I would contribute to labor in the forest and in time my passion for running vanished.

The period following halting my education I found myself and my mother working hand and hand supporting our family which was not easy for me either. I hated the inquisitive nature of the community members asking why I am not at school. I felt embarrassed resulting to hiding from general public.

For another few years worked in this forest where I met ruthless individuals. We would work together at times just to end up with zero pennies. There were bully's and abusers of all sorts; a notorious individual named Waithaka from Meru posed a significant threat. He had missed an opportunity to torture me few years back after my rite of passage and now I was freely available in his domain; even though he wasn't sure if I was circumcised or not; he delved in the believe that he cannot be working in the same field with uncircumcised man. He needed clarification and also his share of cigarettes and if I am still uncut he and his peers would perform the cut themselves.

He had bided his time until my return to work in the forest, seizing the opportunity to torment and torture me in the absence of our boss. I would diligently collect wood for my pile, only to find it stolen by Waithaka to bolster his own collection. I confronted him and of course that was the time he was waiting. Our altercation led to permanent animosity

***

The next one year I work in various jobs for the same man who was my counselor. I worked in his farms picking coffee and tea leaves where I later ran away from his employment due to hardships that were beyond my humility.

I tried all way to make a living even running way from home to live with distance friends. My mother sought my whereabouts and finally confronted. Breaking new great news from my aunt in Nairobi, she summoned me to come home immediately as my aunt will come to pick me the next day for a job position in Nairobi. As a young boy this was unheard off.

Unbeknownst to us, one of my aunts had approached my dad with a proposal, she asked for my school certificates to secure me a job in the city. Upon her receiving my certificates and the title deed for our land; he secures a loan for establishing a business focused on selling and distributing books to schools. In return he secured an employment for me in the city. At this early age I found myself en route to Nairobi city. Our arrival took place on a Sunday night, and by the following day, I was already working at a ceramic factory in the heart of the city where my uncle was chief accountant. In the book "Mandelitta", it accounts my short life in hell and my return home. In the book it highlights my suffering in the bursting streets on Nairobi where my aunt sought an opportunity to monetarize our assets as a means of emancipating us from extreme poverty. My employment didn't last long; at the end of my turmoils in the city and a sense of shame on my face it reached a point to bid goodbye to city life and was back to the same poverty infested lifestyle. By the time I exit the city I had lost my nation identity card and I never got by my education certificates from my uncle though for several years he alluded to have given them back to me after the employment.

Frustrated by these ongoing challenges, I realized life trajectory wasn't on my best favor. I dreaded my youthful age and my love for running in early school times. I wanted to do something different than anyone else. Whatever I missed; my break from school was all in my mind and there was a need to get re-started and for this reason it started re-manifesting itself in me. Intermittently I started reading anything and every book that come my way. Over time I crept back to books; attending the library and enrolling to studying correspondences which provided enough material to study. It was unusual at my time to study from home while receiving study materials from post office. Ironically, I would spend much of the day hours with my peers but once I go back home I would bury my head on books. All my nights were filled with studies. I never miss newspaper magazine for current news as my dad brough in Newspapers from work every day and they become my escape from the evening and night out with my peers.

From these newspapers I admired athletics columns and results. I came to know some of the top running names from newspapers with their performance's photos taking me by storm as I dreaded to be just like them.

Meanwhile I approached one of the neighbors who was in a boxing club doubling with running. I told him my desire for sport and in particular running. In recollection whatever I desire as my destiny become a nostalgic reminisce in my memory.

Francis Ndwigah was well known in the community as a go getter. Several years after Stephen fame had disappeared, Francis did everything to stand out from the community as a sports wannabe. Everyone admired him and no one remembered Stephen. I source my running guidance from Francis who was very generous in deed. Francis offered some basics of fitness and advised me to find other sports to make maintain my fitness before the releases of yearly calendar by Athletic Kenya (previously K A.A A).

I was happy to join a group of young soccer players and I played in number eleven. We played with various teams but chances of walking out with injuries increased as we advanced. Even locally I would not enjoy the idea of walking home limping or with negative feelings every day after training. After several months of engaging in soccer it was time to say goodbye as I delved into active running season.

Francis being my mentor showed me the short route he ran every morning before going to work. He would wake up at six on the morning and finished the five-kilometer loop before embarking to his secular job. I tried his formula and was a little shy to do it due to how peoples commented and spoke about my new endeavor. I ended up running only in the forest where no one from my village saw whatever stunts I was engaging in. That year I participated in my first community open cross country run finishing thirty-four out of over one hundred and ten runners. It was twelve kilometers route and fifty-eight minutes was good time for me. I was surprised that even without proper training and with minimal guidance I finished the event leaving more than half of participants behind me.

I had no running shoes and Francis would offer me his used shoes. Some were way out of their balance but I had no other way to keep myself from injuries. I remember one type of shoe that that had rigid sole and wasn't good for running at all. I ended up with a severe injury that forced me to take time off from training. Francis encouraged me to continue training the next one year so that I can build my endurance and also get to know who is who in running circles. He also introduced me to Charles Gitau, a remarkable police officer who become one of my pillars of my career development. Charles held National record for eight-hundred meters; doubled it with the High School championships at the time. Also, he held East African Police Championships and the Kenyan Police Championships record for eight hundred meters for many years. His record stood fourth fastest in National performance of all time. He also loved running cross-country. Charles carried and composed demeanor and was very well educated. He also prayed valley ball during off season. My engagement with Charles within sports realm gave me a chance to learn how to endure running pains, how to control weight and when to start preparing for an active season.

The following year with newer and more friends to run with I did much better while my friend Francis won the Embu District cross-country championship. I finished top ten and two week later Eastern province championships were held where I finished sixth in the junior category behind Mumo Muindi, Cosmas Ndeti, Atoi Boru, Jimmy Muindi, and Daniel Mutuiri. All those runners had better training and coaching brains behind them. I advanced to the national championships where name swap happened. That was when I realized that inequality existed everywhere and, in all forms, including sporting events. The names of Atoi Boru, Daniel Mutwiri and myself were replaced with others who didn't compete at provincial levels. The unfortunate truth was that those names were not swapped were runners who were from Machakos District (Today Machakos County). During the nationals, Andrew Maasai and Paul Kipkoech won the twelve kilometers race respectively while Mumo, Jimmy, Cosmas finished top eight in junior category and advanced to World Cross Country. I admired their performances at the national level. Advancing to the national participation in my first attempt left me fascinated. Despite name swapping I promised myself to do much better the following year.

***

The year was nineteen-nighty-eight when I decided to explore more into running. The same year Kenya inter-municipality Sports and Cultural (Kimsca) association festivals were to be held in my home town. Embu Municipality required performances on all fraternities. We had a chance to showcase ourselves and potentially get employment by then social service officer who was in charge of sports administration. M/s Mate would come to the track every evening to watch how her team was training and perhaps recruit new sportsmen for her municipality. For several weeks she followed our training and even took us to weekend meetings. Within three months she had identified me as one to represent her municipality in ten thousand meters, five thousand meter and any other sports that I felt comfortable participating in during the one-week festival.

During the games in Embu I ran five thousand meters in fifteen minutes and forty-five seconds finishing fifth. It was impressive because top six runners carried reversed points for your team. This particular event stood out to me because it was my first sporting festival that I had was involved with featuring a residential camping, wearing full tracksuits uniforms bearing the names of the municipality one represented. I also remember borrowing a Walkman from my close friend Levis Irungu. Having a Walkman during that time provided a spectacular moment of adorned from your peers. The sporting event ended with my name appearing to top performance at the municipalities but there was no extended benefit to this participation.

The next year I increased my training exponentially as long as I was not getting injured. If I feel like running three of four times a day I did just that. My l running fanatic saw me even waking up at odd times for lack of a watch. I remember one day waking up and walking a twenty minutes distance to wake up my two new running friends in my neighborhood. Though they complained because we all collectively had no watches to tell us what time it was, they resolved accepting my call. We ran for fifty minutes and came back home while it was still dark and dead quiet. We slept for more hours before morning. During the day they told me never to ever wake them up for training and if I want to run that late, I am free to do it on my own. I gauged my running with my energy levels at any given moment. Anything above enough energy to walk was enough to make me jump up and run. Ironically, I ate very little food since there was nothing at home. I chewed sugarcane all day and every time I felt hungry, I would feed on cassava that I would get from my grandfather's land which bush had overgrown since his demise.

The following year Kimsca games were held in Meru. About ninety kilometers from Embu. Still representing Embu municipality, I had a chance to participate in multiple events; fifteen hundred meters, five thousand meters and three thousand meters Steeple Chase. I did not embrace steeple chase because clearing the water obstacle was very tough for me. I finished 3rd in 1500m with 3.55sec, second in 5000m in 15.15 sec and second in steeplechase in 9 minutes and thirty-eight seconds. It was another milestone for me and remains one of my breakthrough moments.

Back in Embu my training resumed amplifying my spirit for running. I found myself running with everyone and mixed training planned had their own impact on me. Nursing injuries become the new normal. For some reason the devil knows his ways to lure innocent people astray; while soothing my running injuries my neighbor who had a small restaurant in a place called Wango coerced me to work for him telling me that it wise to find something to do for myself instead of running aimlessly. He rebuked the notion of success in running telling me I will die poor if I think I will get anything from my aimless running. His conviction compelled me to join him and work for him; his business was a few kilometers off Karaba Market in Mwea area which is 20 kilometers further interior from the main road that runs from Embu to Nairobi.

For another year I worked relentless for this man, I did everything including cooking and preparing tea and coffee; fetching water as far as Masinga dam, going to the farms to buy firewood and charcoal. Keeping the café well managed. During that time running was forgotten. He left me after six months to manage the place just visiting every two months. After another eight months I informed him my desire to go home to see my parents and needed my pay. Astonishingly he handed me two hundred and eighty shillings and told me he will give me the rest on my return as he has just renewed the licenses to operate his business. The money he gave me was less than one month's pay after relentlessly working for eight months. I visited home and returned with hopes of getting my remaining pay. Sadly, I had to accrue more to get paid for that was owed to me. I opted leaving his job and whatever he owed me and find anything else to do.

I got a job at the Catholic mission construction site; worked there for two months and they offered me to relocate to another site at Makutano Mwea twenty-five kilometers away at the main road to the Nairobi city. This was a new project constructing Wachoro Secondary School. I reported on day one. We slept on the same construction site as we started ground breaking on the new site, then laying slap and the mounting of the walls. There I learned how to balance the level stones and aligning them to elect a classroom walls, how to mix and install mortar, cementing and point finishing. I worked there for another several months.

The contract job at Wachoro didn't last forever; our services to the site ended after several months and I found myself grappling on my next course of action. For few weeks I sought any jobs within Mwea proximities. I would join fishermen at Masinga dam at dawn, spent the rest of the day hanging around with new friend until my energy to stay put wore down.

I visited Wango once more to find new opportunities that might have emerged. One of the people I knew required some handyman to assist him to complete his house; I was ready to tackle this job because I had gained a lot of building skills from my previous job. We agreed on the payment rate and the next few days I was busy helping him. I stayed in one of his cubes he had build as a store.

After few months my health took a different turn. I had developed chronic malaria from drinking unclean water. The illness symptoms were psychotic in nature.

The brain with generate continuous rhetoric while trying to give answers to the same simultaneously. I found my brain full occupied whenever I was awake. Lying down increased my heart beat and raced increasingly high causing some dizziness. This went on for several days. One afternoon I realized that I am really sick and I might collapse any minute. Any attempt to do any work failed. I had no time to wait for my master; I was compelled to informed the wife that I am unwell and need to go to the hospital. I made quick decision that if I am to die its better to die closer to my family. My family is poor and for me to die this far means plunging my family in more problems. I made my decision that I will die at home or at least not this far. Summoning the courage to broach the subject with my host, I requested the compensation owed to me, knowing that time was of the essence.

Her response, though not ideal, offcred a glimmer of hope. She handed me whatever she had at the moment though not what I had worked for; I accepted the amount, knowing it would suffice for my journey home, albeit with a considerable distance to traverse on foot before I could secure a ride.

I left with nothing but bus fare; destination Embu general hospital.

As I contemplated my uncertain fate, one thought resonated deeply within me: the desire to bid farewell to my family, especially my beloved mother, before my time on this earth reached its end. She had been my pillar of strength, my unwavering source of support throughout my struggles, and I longed for one last opportunity to express my gratitude and love.

With heartfelt farewells exchanged in mind, I set out on the arduous trek, carrying nothing but the wisdom imparted by my mother: she always advised me to carry a piece of paper bearing my essential details: full name, address, and parentage should the need arise. As I ventured towards Karaba market, familiar faces crossed my path, each questioning my departure from the usual route towards Wango at this time of the day which seemed unusual. My vague response about running errands seemed to satisfy their curiosity, allowing me to continue undisturbed.

***

After a grueling forty-five minutes' walk, I finally reached Karaba shopping center. Knowing that public transportation ceased after 6 p.m., I scanned the horizon for any sign of passing vehicles. The only ones that occasionally traversed the road were Catholic diocesan vehicles ferrying Fathers for missions and were never allowed to carry any unauthorized persons, Cotton Board Corporation Land Cruisers returning from field work and were at full capacity and the Kenya Electricity Generating Company Landcruisers. At times all these vehicles served as rescue amenities to anyone in distress at this remote area. However, there seemed to be no urgent need for their services at the moment, leaving me with limited options. Private lorries laden with relief food passed by, but none were bound for my destination. With time ticking away, I resigned myself to the inevitable and prepared for another ten-kilometer trek ahead to the main road.

As I treaded along the deserted road, the isolation overshadowed my physical discomfort. This is the place that roads clear by six-thirty in the evening. Despite my ailment, the potential vulnerability of being targeted by muggers crept into my thoughts. After all, I bore no visible indicators of my condition, leaving me just as susceptible as any other passerby. To the opportunistic thief, anything I possessed no matter how insignificant it is to me, it held value to the mugger. This realization heightened my sense of vulnerability, yet I pressed on, determined to reach my destination unscathed.

After other hour of walk, I reached the tarmac road; darkness had enveloped the landscape. The few small shops lining the roadside stood silent and deserted, their doors left wide open as a precaution against theft. It was a common practice for shop owners to clear out their merchandise before nightfall, knowing that leaving anything behind would invite pilfering overnight. Some even opted to leave their doors ajar, signaling to potential thieves that there was nothing of value left to plunder inside.

As I cautiously approached the shops, I detected the faint murmur of male voices having a deep argument emanating from within, signaling the presence of others nearby. I made sure no one noticed my presence.

***

I paused to eavesdrop on the conversation unfolding before me. Voices rose in heated argument, of which I wasn't sure of the subject but I was sure they were unfriendly people therefore I made sure I had to avoid exposing myself to them. Silently, I navigated my way to the other side of the road, concealing myself amidst the untamed landscape until I reached the edge of the tarmac.

Suddenly, a glimmer of light pierced the darkness, heralding the arrival of a Nissan matatu from Nairobi. Seizing the opportunity as it stopped to drop a traveler, I approached the vehicle hastily, inquiring if they were bound for Embu. The conductor's response was terse and urgent, warning of the imminent danger lurking in this "red zone" and insisting on prompt payment.

As the conductor spoke, the sound of whistling and shouting grew louder, signaling the approach of an unknown group of youths. With a sense of urgency, the driver threatened to depart without the conductor if any further delay ensued. In a swift motion, the conductor ushered me aboard, demanding payment under the threat of expulsion onto the unforgiving road.

I quickly surrendered the money I had prepared in advance, ensuring my place onboard. An hour later, the matatu came to a halt near Embu General Hospital, the clock striking nine in the evening; making my way to the main registration bay, I exchanged my last twenty shillings for an outpatient medical card, then proceeded to the outpatient department only to find the doctor's queue overflowing with weary patients.

To my dismay, I discovered that the night doctor was egregiously late, delaying the start of his duties by a staggering four hours. The absence of the evening doctor, who had vanished after a brief after he reported to work left a trail of frustration and exhaustion among the waiting patients, some of whom had endured a five-hour ordeal without respite.

Faced with the prospect of a prolonged wait, hunger gnawing at my stomach, I resolved to make the journey to my parents' home, located three kilometers northwest from the hospital.

As I set out into the night, a profound stillness engulfed the world around me, offering a stark contrast to the chaos and uncertainty of the hours prior.

The journey stretched on, the darkness of the night shrouding my surroundings as I pressed forward. Upon my arrival home, the late hour had already enveloped the household in slumber. However, my mother's intuition seemed to stir as I entered, her welcoming presented a beacon of comfort amidst the uncertainty. Despite the late hour, her warm embrace and tender words invigorated me in a sense of security, reminding me of the unwavering love that anchored me to my roots.

***

At home I was met with a mix of emotions—joy and relief from my family, yet also the worry and anguish of parents seeing their child unwell. It was late at night, and I returned home in a sorry state, my pockets empty and my health deteriorating. I wasted no time in informing my parents of my condition, conveying my urgent need for their assistance. Unfortunately, my father seemed somewhat detached, his concern overshadowed by his frustration with my recent erratic behavior.

Thankfully, my mother sprang into action, immediately summoning my younger brother to accompany us to the hospital. Once at the hospital, a battery of tests was conducted to diagnose my illness, the results revealing a troubling combination of malaria, typhoid, and anxiety. The doctor wasted no time in prescribing a course of treatment, which commenced with two injections administered that very night, followed by a regimen of repeat injections every other day. Unfortunately, the pharmacy was closed by the time we left the hospital, necessitating a return trip the following day to procure the necessary medications.

By the time we returned home in the early hours of the morning, exhaustion weighed heavily upon me, and I retreated to bed, succumbing to much-needed rest. The following day passed in a blur of sleep and wakefulness, as my mother assumed the role of caretaker, tirelessly seeking out resources to purchase the medications essential for my recovery.

The ensuing three months unfolded as a harrowing chapter in my life, marked by scarcity and deprivation. With each passing day, the specter of hunger loomed large, our meals growing increasingly meager and inadequate. This dire circumstance rendered even the most potent medications ineffectual, their palliative effects flecting against the backdrop of relentless hunger and malnutrition. Though the medication offered temporary respite, my illness persisted, its grip on my weakened body tightening with each passing day.

As my physical condition deteriorated, my mental state began to fray at the edges, my mind besieged by a relentless barrage of questions and uncertainties. It felt as though my brain had taken on a life of its own, its incessant questioning echoing loudly within the confines of my consciousness. In a surreal and disorienting experience, I found myself engaged in a bizarre dialogue with my own mind, as though attempting to reason with a relentless interrogator.

As I struggled to grapple with this inner turmoil, a profound weariness settled over me, my energy depleted by the ceaseless mental gymnastics. I became acutely aware of my precarious state, the gnawing hunger and cognitive dissonance serving as stark reminders of the dire circumstances in which I found myself. Despite my best efforts to conceal my plight from those around me, I couldn't shake the feeling of vulnerability, the fear that my internal struggles might manifest themselves in ways beyond my control.

Week after week, I found myself returning to the same doctor, grappling with the relentless grip of an ailment that refused to relent. The diagnosis revealed a grim reality – chronic malaria had entrenched itself within me, resisting the effects of various treatments, including the notorious quinine, a name that sent shivers down the spine of those who had encountered its reactions that trigger a ring of bells on one's eardrum. There were rumors that this drug may cause deafness.

Amidst the desperation, a pivotal moment arose when the doctor, in an act of last resort, prescribed Fansider; a three-tablet dosage. The doctor thought that this medicine carries a promising potential salvation. Eager for relief, I acquired the medication in town and due to the intense pain, consumed it immediately. As I journeyed back home, I paused by at a longtime friend in the neighborhood where my old friend Patrick engaged in a spirited game of draft with fellow mates. Resting there, I inadvertently succumbed to sleep on a chair. The tranquility was shattered when I awoke to my own anguished screams and violent jerking. The burning sensation in my feet escalated into a tormenting sequence of intervals, culminating in a sharp explosion of pain centered at my heart. Startled, my friends didn't know what to do but some opted disperse in case something happens with me leaving only a few courageous men by my side.

Concerned, they inquired about the source of my distress and what I had consumed that day. Recounting my recent hospital visit and the prescribed medication, they unanimously decided to escort me back to seek urgent medical attention. The journey to the hospital was marked by my sporadic convulsions, alarming everyone we encountered along the way.

Arriving at the hospital, an air of urgency surrounded my admission. Laid on the doctor's table, my papers scrutinized, the attending physician delivered a somber verdict; the medication had triggered a reaction, rendering further treatment perilous given the distressed state of my heart. Left with no alternative, I lay there, the hospital becoming an unwitting witness to a battle between life and the looming specter of mortality.

An agonizing hour later, the fiery pain subsided, and the screams were replaced by an eerie silence. The physician called one of the friends who were waiting outside and instructed him to take me home and make sure that I had food before too long. Together, we embarked on the solemn walk back home, the night bearing witness to the tumultuous ordeal that had unfolded.

The next few weeks I nursed myself with meager resources; I desired quick recovery and return of my energy. Burdened by a multitude of pills ranging from 9 to 17, three times a day. Nutrition posed a significant challenge, with meager offerings from the depleted farmland, devoid of essential manure or fertilizers. Each passing day found me growing weaker, teetering ever closer to the brink.

Amidst the turmoil of my health struggles and with my sickly status, I visited one fellow runner who lived within Embu town. His whispers were the grapevine that the Kenya Post and Telecommunication sector had a mass recruitment drive, seeking only the top three runners in every event to join their ranks who are now basking in the privileges of paid athletes. All this happened when I wasted my ample time cooking donuts and teas to ungrateful employer.

The bitter pill of disappointment lodged in my throat as I grappled with the unfairness of it all. How could those athletes, many of whom I had outrun countless times, now revel in success while I languished in weakness and failure? In a moment of self-reflection, I confronted my own inadequacies. Weak and unremarkable, I lacked the very qualities that would make me competitive in the job market. My national identity card, a crucial document for employment, was lost somewhere in the bustling streets of the city. As for my school certificates, they too were a distant memory, entrusted to my aunt in a hopeful bid to secure a job opportunity in the urban sprawl.

The harsh reality dawned on me; I was ill-prepared and ill-equipped for the challenges that lay ahead. With each passing day, the weight of my destitution bore down on me, casting doubt on any aspirations of a brighter future. It became painfully clear that I faced a daunting uphill battle, a series of arduous steps that needed to be taken before even a glimmer of progress could emerge from the depths of my despair.

In the solitude of my thoughts, I grappled with the notion that perhaps fate had dealt me a cruel hand, condemning me to a life of perpetual struggle and unfulfilled dreams. Yet, deep within me, a flicker of determination persisted;

a stubborn resolve to defy the odds and carve out a path of my own, no matter how rugged or unforgiving it may be.

***

Frail and feeble, I began to confront the inevitable reality of my own mortality. Each evening, I sought solace in the company of my mother, clinging to the hope that I would awaken to see her once more in the morning.

Despite my best efforts to find respite in sleep, my body rebelled against any attempt to rest. Lying down only served to intensify my discomfort, my heart rate escalating with each passing moment. A peculiar snapping sound echoed within my nostrils, a disconcerting reminder of the underlying turmoil within my body. Days blurred into nights as I grappled with the enigma of my deteriorating health, desperate for answers that remained agonizingly elusive.

My younger sister was unfamiliar with the version of me that existed before her time. Often, she would regale me with anecdotes and tales of a brother who had departed long time ago when she was a little girl; she hoped the brother would come home while

I am still around so that I can meet him. Oblivious to the fact that she was recounting stories about me, she spoke freely, unaware of the connection until several weeks had passed. It was then that her memory pieced together the fragments, realizing that the brother she spoke of was none other than myself. This made me feel sad that I am ailing and might even die before my sister enjoyed much time with the runaway brother she cared about.

In my frail state, I found myself contemplating the inevitable, envisioning the grave side resting place of my grandfather. Would I join him in eternal slumber, side by side, or would there be a solitary gap between our graves, awaiting the arrival of my gland mother was still alive? Each evening, I sought solace in the company of my mother, clinging to the hope of another dawn.

As night yielded to day, my mother's presence became a constant reassurance, a beacon of comfort in the darkness. Without fail, before the sun could cast its first light upon the horizon, she would appear at my hut, a silent sentinel of care and concern; hopeful I did not die overnight.

Day in day out I would spend some hours with my grandmother who entertained me with the good, the bad and the ugly of everything in life while teaching me how to weave homemade wooden trays. Cow waste was the finishing touch smeared well both inside and out. It turned out that in her generation use of cow refuse was a protective product against weevils. But her creative work fell off the market with arrival of conventional plastics trays.

She had other side of the stories; her hellbent perceptions of my own mother as the cause of my illness alluding to witchcraft practices; the poor state our family a result from my mother's secret religion sect. Other times she would narrate era she called "majeneti" (emergency) and life after the British colonial emergency declaration, the detention of the African men; the Mau Mau tribulations and the pre-independent mass confinements in what they termed as Gichagi "Village" that were guarded overnight and none movement curfews imposed between six o'clock in the evening and six in the morning.

It was the time to learn who bore the blood of their African kins against the white rulers who come in form of Christians. Its was time to grow as a man and discern the truth and trash other mystic stories.

***

Devoid of a place to call home and lacking purpose in my life, the specter of starvation loomed large, threatening to engulf me at any moment. My body bore the unmistakable marks of deprivation, its once vibrant hue faded to a pallid, ashen shade. With muscles wasting away and eyes sunken into my hollowed face, I found myself adrift in a sea of isolation, bereft of the solace that companionship could bring.

In the desolation of my existence, I came to a sobering realization: my presence held little significance to anyone beyond the confines of my immediate family.

Faced with the stark truth of my insignificance in the world, I resolved to bid farewell to my family while I still retained the ability to speak.

Before I utter my desperation to live any longer to my family and in the recesses of my mind, a vague recollection stirred; an idea whispered by a friend whose identity remained elusive in my memory. They had spoken of the therapeutic power of sports and natural remedies in common ailments, this was a passive story of engaging in a spirited debate among our circle of friends some years earlier. Though the discussion wasn't directly aimed at me, this time my memories refreshed and I deliberated on it. I felt a need to try this remedy of hope as an alternative approach. With conventional medications proving ineffective against my myriad of illnesses, I found myself at a crossroads. Weak and deprived of sustenance, I hesitated. Yet, driven by desperation and a sliver of optimism, I resolved to embark on this uncharted path of self-discovery and experimentation. I rationalized that even if I were to succumb to the trial, my legacy would be one of defiance; choosing to face my demise head-on, rather than succumbing to the slow decay of my current state.

Living with a persistent headache that refused to relent, I found myself in a dire state. My heart palpitated randomly several times a day. My mind became a battleground, where questions seemed to materialize out of thin air, echoing within the chambers of my consciousness; my brain generated questions that sounded audible to me. In a surreal dance, I would attempt to respond to these phantom inquiries, only for my thoughts to spiral into an endless loop of interrogation endlessly. I become very weary trying to scan and see if anyone near me would notice what I am going through. I realized this is only inside my brain. This was my last state of a sober mind that I possess and I become aware that anything beyond this was fatal.

Fortunately, our proximity to the forest offered me a lifeline. With just a three-minute journey, I began venturing into the lush greenery to embark on my newfound regimen of running. Initially, I started with a modest routine, jogging through the forest. Remarkably, after just three days of the first week, I noticed a reduction in the intensity of my headaches, although they persisted. Encouraged by this progress, I decided to push myself further in the second week, increasing the frequency of my runs to every day. To my astonishment, by the end of that second week, my chronic headache vanished completely, never to return. In a moment of triumph, I made the bold decision to cease taking all the medications that had been prescribed to me, finding solace and healing in the rhythm of my daily runs amidst the serene embrace of the forest.

After the first month, I was experiencing a remarkable improvement in my health, albeit still weakened by malnutrition. Running had become more than just a routine; it felt like my destiny and a fundamental part of my existence. Embracing the positive trajectory my health had taken, I persisted in my newfound passion for running, eagerly immersing myself in its benefits. I even began joining my old friends who had long been reaping the rewards of regular exercise. Francis, in particular, had made significant strides, securing a job in the military and successfully completing his training. During his off days, he would visit me, offering words of encouragement and discussing potential employment opportunities that lay ahead for me. His unwavering support bolstered my confidence and fueled my determination to continue on my journey towards better health and a brighter future.

That year, I competed in cross country races, gradually advancing until I reached the national level. Despite the challenges posed by my previous illness, I managed to finish in the top hundred, a feat that left me pleasantly surprised. Just one week after the national championships, rumors began circulating about a potential repeat recruitment drive by Kenya Post and Telecommunications. Excited by the prospect of this opportunity, I was able to improve my own time distances on all routes that I was training on; I was prepared for this event.

However, three days before the scheduled recruitment drive, disaster struck. I awoke to excruciating pain radiating from my right fibula bone, accompanied by visible inflammation. Every attempt to run only intensified the agony, leaving me incapacitated and unable to showcase my running talent as I had hoped. Despite my injury, I resolved to attend the recruitment event, clinging to the hope that perhaps I could still participate or that someone familiar with my abilities might advocate on my behalf.

Throughout the event, I made several futile attempts to join in when the running events were announced. However, each time I attempted to warm up, the familiar pain flared up within minutes, dashing any hopes of demonstrating my capabilities.

Though I had missed a great chance for employment, I still enjoyed watching those who were able to run effectively securing their jobs. I convinced myself there will be another recruiting drive that will find me in better running conditions.

My recovery journey has been long and arduous, marked by the diligent application of home remedies to alleviate my pain. I vividly recall the days spent burning the inflamed area with various objects, seeking relief from the persistent discomfort. I did this because I could not afford sports injury treatment or pain reliever. Despite these efforts, it wasn't until I began visiting the Embu Physiotherapy Clinic for ultrasound treatments that I started to notice significant improvements.

However, my progress hit a snag when my visits to the clinic became less frequent due to scheduling conflicts and staff shortages. Undeterred, I took matters into my own hands and devised alternative methods for treatment. I turned to heated banana peels and lantern lamps to soothe my injuries, a makeshift solution that I persisted with for several months. I also used stinging nettle to burn the inflamed area and if lucky getting Ice from butcheries

Through sheer determination and perseverance, I eventually regained my strength and mobility. With my injuries healed, I eagerly returned to the track, rejoining my training friends at the Embu Stadium. It was a triumphant moment, marking the culmination of my resilience and the beginning of a new chapter in my running journey.

That year marked a significant shift in my training regimen as I intensified my efforts, transitioning from one training session per day to two. Drawing inspiration from senior runners, I observed their techniques and strategies, adapting them to align with my own goals and aspirations.

In my quest for success, I sought guidance from my friend Francis, who graciously provided me with the annual calendar of events organized by the Kenya Amateur Athletics Association (KAAA), now known as Athletics Kenya. He emphasized the importance of seizing opportunities early, highlighting the significance of the first three regional cross-country meets.

Francis revealed a valuable insider tip: the top ten runners from these initial three cross county meetings are closely monitored and considered for international invitations in the subsequent months of February, March, April, and May. It was a breakthrough revelation, known to only a select few in the running community.

Armed with this newfound knowledge, I intensified my training, directing my focus towards excelling in the upcoming meets. With each stride, I aimed to position myself among the elite contenders, eager to seize the opportunities that lay ahead.

***

Amidst the tumultuous events unfolding in my life, I cherished the enduring friendships I had cultivated since my early days. Among these companions was Dan Muchoki, a figure of great renown in the world of Kenyan athletics. As Kenya's National Coach boasting IAAF certifications, Dan commanded respect both nationally and internationally; a sentiment I shared. Luckily Dan was from my home town, Embu. A small town occasionally inundated with few foreigners and government officials. Embu commands a great presence of high schools with student coming from all over the country. Perhaps because of it altitude, average temperatures and its peaceful grounds.

I made it a point to cultivate a relationship with Dan, eagerly seeking his guidance during the days he devoted to training athletes at the Embu stadium. Initially, approaching him amidst a throng of accomplished runners was no easy feat. However, fortune smiled upon me when Dan expressed interest in my background.

Dan, recognizing the potential within each of us, issued a challenge to strive for excellence, promising his support and guidance as a senior figure within the sports administration. His encouragement spurred me on, fueling my determination to pursue my athletic ambitions with renewed vigor.

Now and then I would look for Dan when he is in town, find where he is enjoying his favorite beer talking to his elite class and well-versed base with day and day activities of Embu town. Once surrounded by a streak of runners seeking his guidance, the real sports conversation would erupt; one by one he would offer insight to every individual based on their recent performances. One day Dan challenged me asking the reason for not performing well in the recent events. I alluded that the other runners were faster, stronger and maybe more talented than I was. His rhetoric left me in embarrassments; Dan would retorted stating "who among them did you find having three legs; tell me whom among them who you realized having two hearts!",

In a stroke of serendipity, the Kenyan world cross-country team was slated to undergo a three-week residential training program at Embu St. Mark's Teachers College. Through the graciousness of Dan Muchoki, we were afforded the opportunity to visit the team and observe their training sessions. It was during this time that I had the privilege of meeting some of Kenya's most illustrious athletes, including John Ngugi, a legendary figure in cross-country running who had clinched the world title five times, with four consecutive victories. Moses Tanui among others I also encountered Jane and Margaret Ngotho, two exceptional sisters renowned for their running prowess, along with Waithera and other esteemed runners.

As the training program drew to a close, Dan approached me and another young athlete with a special offer. He invited us to accompany the team to the airport to see the team off as they embarked on their journey to compete in the World Championships in Aix-les-Bains, France, at the prestigious Hippodrome de Marlioz. It was an honor beyond measure to be offered such a moment, and I eagerly seized the opportunity to be part of this momentous occasion. Some military officer had requested Dan to get them young upcoming runners to train with their runners as they wait for military recruitments. This was a shorter route to join the military ranks. I asked my mother for pocket money as I endeavor into this open world.

After attending to the team's travel arrangements at Nyayo Stadium, we made our way to the city center for their banquet prior to their flight and subsequent departure to the airport. Among the group was Dan Muchoki, who left instructions for us to be taken to the Military Training Camp at Ngong the following day. After the team's departure the college driver who drove us to police hostels at Kasarani police base where we spent the night in anticipation of the next day's instructions.

True to Dan's instructions, a military officer arrived the following day to escort us to the Roysambu training camp within the city. There, we were to await further instructions from Dan. However, the military coaches decided to proceed with Dan's directive and transported us to Ngong training camp. Covered in a military truck, our view obscured, we traversed the city until we arrived at the Ngong military sports training venue approximately an hour later.

Upon our arrival, we found no permanent housing structures, only tents, most of which were unoccupied. It appeared that the military sportsmen had taken a hiatus after the national championship to spend time with their families. We were shown two tents where each of us could choose which one to sleep in. For three days, we resided there peacefully, running everyday with the few officers who had remained at the camp.

However, on the third day, the atmosphere shifted dramatically. The military runners returned one by one to find us occupying their beds, and their reaction was one of vocal arrogance. They demanded to know who had granted us permission to sleep in their beds, questioning whether any of us had brought our own bedding or where we expected to sleep if not in our own accommodations.

That evening, we received the disheartening news that there was no space available for us at the camp. Furthermore, it was made clear that Dan, despite his esteemed position, lacked the authority of a military officer to issue directives within the military realm. It was a sobering realization of the limitations we faced in navigating the intricate hierarchy of military protocol.

***

I returned by to my home for yet another chapter. Training was my main focus and daily task. It turned out that every time I geared up for rigorous training, gearing myself mentally and physically for the upcoming challenge, fate had other plans. As the days drew closer to the any race, I would encounter some impediments: illness, lack of transportation, and distant meetings that seemed impossible to attend. While the distance itself wasn't insurmountable, lacking reliable means of transport compounded the challenge. But sickness proved the most formidable adversary, halting my preparations in their tracks. Often, just days before my scheduled departure, illness would strike, bringing my spirits crashing down.

In the aftermath of the adversity that befell us, I found myself drawn to the needs of my own mother. In the midst of poverty's grip, solidarity became our lifeline, and the unity of our family was paramount. It dawned on me that while I pursued my passion for running, my family toiled tirelessly in the fields, striving to secure our sustenance which I hand abandoned to pursue my running career.

A sense of unease gnawed at me, as if I were a burden weighing heavily on my mother's heart, and I yearned for her unconditional blessing. Determined to bridge the gap between us, I seized an opportunity one afternoon to have a heart-to-heart with her. Sitting together, I embarked on a conversation that I hoped would strengthen our bond and reassure her of my devotion to our family's well-being.

With a heavy heart, I began my earnest conversation with my dear mother, pouring out my struggles and frustrations. "I've been grappling to fulfill my running aspirations, but I find myself caught in a whirlwind of illness and circumstantial setbacks," I explained to my mother lamenting. "Injuries strike at crucial moments, and I lack the means to travel to pivotal events that could potentially change our lives forever."

As I spoke, I endeavored to convey to my mother the profound impact that my running could have on our entire family's future. While she possessed some understanding of the significance of sports, the intricacies of my endeavor remained unfamiliar to her. Seeking her understanding and forgiveness for any shortcomings on my part, I implored her for her blessings, recognizing that her support could be the key to unlocking my destiny.

"I need your openness and forgiveness," I concluded, my plea tinged with hope and desperation. Gazing into my mother's eyes, I awaited her response with bated breath. Finally, she spoke, her words carrying the weight of her maternal love and acceptance. "I harbor no ill feelings toward you, and I wish you success in your pursuit," she said, her words a beacon of encouragement in the midst of uncertainty.

Just few weeks after my conversation with my mother on a Saturday, that day my dad didn't g anywhere as usual, he stayed home. A neighbor who worked in town come with a newspaper and handed it to my dad. This was shocking news; our only piece of land was again this being the third time to be auctioned; it was to happen the coming few days. This was the time the truth about what transpired between my dad and my aunt was revealed to me. The time she took me to the city of Nairobi, she had lured her brother (my dad) into releasing the land title deed to her to secure a loan which she defaulted and thus causing the land to be auctioned. This eventful news shock the entire family.

I took this very offensive act personal and proclaimed to my heart that in case we lose our land from this dubious deal, I declared in my heart that one day I will indeed buy land for my parent to re-pay my involvement if there was any.

Luckily with various people's involvement into this consequential event which would have left us homeless and into the streets, the land was never auctioned. I remember this was credited to two people in their generosity; a neighbor called Njoroge wa Nguri through my mums request took his influence to the District Commissioner to halt the auction while my dad sought formula to pay the loan, however my dad had to pay auctioneer's fee; the second person was an uncle married to my dad's sister who paid the entire banks loan. At that moment we were save from eviction but we still owed him his money which took another eight years before paying him back

***

Following the heartfelt blessings bestowed upon me by my mother I was optimistic and determined; embarking on yet another journey of athletic achievement. It was my second year of continuous training, filled with uncertainty about how I would fare at the next national championships. The realization that most of the top sixty finishers at nationals were elite runners with sports agents representing abroad create another layer of performance pressure. Securing a spot in the top 40, therefore, became not just a personal goal but a strategic necessity. With this knowledge weighing heavily on my mind, I immersed myself once again in my training regimen, determined to elevate my performance to the required level. That year, I once again advanced to the national championship in twelve kilometer cross-country, finishing among the top one hundred competitors with forty-two minutes, not within the expected range.

My training never ceased even after the national championships, I continued relentlessly and with determination.

During this period, Francis, my occasional training partner, made a few visits, inadvertently serving as an evaluator of my progress. One particular day, he urged me to embark on a grueling one-hour-ten-minute run, citing time constraints due to his tight schedule of the day; that day we started running much earlier. Little did I know that Francis was out to test my speed endurance and agility. Later Francis expressed his surprise and admiration for my performance of the day and how he worn himself out while secretly putting me into running trial. His acknowledgment of my potential performances in world stage gave me a renewed sense of confidence and determination. Perhaps if I was aware I was being gauged maybe I would have performed much better. It was a significant milestone in my athletic journey mentally.

Following Francis' revelation, I felt a need to accept that I am on a path to success, I changed my mental focus and started detailed specific training aimed to elevate my status before my peers in my neighborhood and also focus on performing at national level.

At that time my daily morning runs were about sixteen kilometers on a very hilly terrain to be completed by 8.00 am. I would spend the rest of the day working in the forest or at farms for sustainability.

Some other days I would jog to Moi Stadium Embu where I will meet a contingent of runners where volunteering coaches awaited. There I would conceal my earlier training and join them for whatever training they were subjected to. Later I would go home jogging again for lunch and rest. By 5.00 pm I would get out for un specified jog that would depend on my energy levels.

Six months later Francis extended an unexpected invitation that would alter the course of my athletic journey. He offered to take me under his wing at the military, introduced me to the military sports camp where he was training. This opportunity was not just about physical training but also a potential pathway to broader opportunities within the military. Joining him at the 78 Tank Battalion cross-country training camp in Nyahururu presented a chance to not only hone my skills but also reconnect with my roots, as my mother hailed from this area.

The military training camp was a bustling hub of athletics activities, surrounded by other prominent training facilities like the Nanyuki Air Base and Kahawa Garrison. Here, amidst seasoned athletes and rising stars, I absorbed valuable lessons and earned the respect of my peers. As I rubbed shoulders with accomplished figures like Paul Ruto and Moses Kiptanui, Kibet, Boniface Merande and once more Atoi Boru who was a junior competitor at early days. Here I also met other waiting recruits like Christopher Kelong and Philip Tarus.   I realized that my journey was just beginning, filled with promise and potential for growth.

Engaging in military training introduced me to a whole new level of rigor and discipline, surpassing anything I had experienced in Embu. Beyond physical exercises, we were schooled in military protocols, from addressing our seniors to understanding the hierarchy of ranks. Even mealtime followed a strict protocol, dictating who should be served first and who should eat last, with waiting recruits like myself ranking at the bottom. We also shared communal duties, such as fetching water and firewood, cooking, and cleaning the open compound where we lived, devoid of any proper housing.

In a cohort of thirteen waiting recruits, competition for favor from both the staff and the army for future employment was fierce. We were constantly monitored for our character, demeanor, performance, and ability to adhere to standing orders. The initial three months proved to be a steep uphill climb for me, marked by occasional injuries. Yet, the most challenging aspect was the need to conceal any sign of suffering; displaying vulnerability risked dismissal and replacement by another recruit. Some fellow sportsmen showed compassion by lending us their gear, offering their shoes, tracksuits, and T-shirts to support us during training sessions.

Among the sportsmen who left a lasting impression on me was Moses Kiptanui, whose demeanor and humility stood out. Despite his remarkable athletic achievements, he treated me with profound respect. Moses generously shared his wealth of knowledge and running tips, offering invaluable advice on achieving peak performance and managing running-related issues. His modesty was striking, even in the face of comments by his military co-workers about his slender appearance, which some misconstrued as a sign of illness. I learned that one could either prioritize appearance over financial security or vice versa, a lesson that resonated deeply with top runners.

The military cross-country training provided me with an unparalleled experience: a three-hour run through the rugged terrain of Marmanet forest taught us a lesson that lasted for years. On a Saturday morning, we boarded a military truck bound for the forest, where we were unceremoniously dropped off with only vague directions. With the blow of a whistle, the long run commenced, and our journey into the depths of the forest began. Within the first 20 minutes, the group splintered at a junction, torn apart by disagreements over the correct route. I gravitated towards a faction of runners with whom I felt comfortable, only to encounter further dissent and confusion as we progressed deeper into the wilderness.

As disagreements intensified and tempers flared, our group fragmented even further, with some members considering retracing their steps. Lost in the dense undergrowth, devoid of water and direction, our situation grew increasingly precarious. The ominous presence of buffalo dung served as a stark reminder that we are not alone; the potential dangers lurking within the forest. Despite our best efforts to navigate the unfamiliar terrain in deep forest, we found ourselves disoriented and isolated, with only the distant hum of the main road offering a glimmer of hope.

After three arduous hours of trudging through the wilderness, we emerged from the forest, weary and depleted, to find that many of our fellow runners who knew the right route had returned to camp hours earlier. Concern mounted as the realization dawned that several individuals had yet to make it back five hours later. With urgency, the officer in charge mobilized senior officers to embark on a search and rescue mission. Tragically, four runners remained unaccounted for, their decision to abandon their running aspirations and their decision of return to their homes casted a somber shadow over the otherwise triumphant day.

Hill work was done almost punitively. I remember a small hill just few meters from Thompsons Falls we would be subjected to 20 repeats with no exceptions. Bewilderment encircle everyone when Atoi Boru, a world class 1500m and cross country runner who was with second Kenyan army battalion distinctively ran 40 repeats. An attempt what was only done by legendary John Ngugi at the time. The day this workout was shared among us no one dared talk about their agility in hill workouts any more unless one can out-perform that tiny looking world better.

During my stay with the military, I had the opportunity to participate in the several Kenya Amateur Athletics Association (KAAA) meeting under the military observations, However, the closure of the cross-country training camp two months later signaled a shift in our circumstances. We were moved to the Battalion base in Isiolo, situated a four hour drive from Nyahururu town, where we awaited further instructions regarding military recruitment.

***

After spending an additional four months in Isiolo, all waiting recruits, including myself, were unexpectedly sent home and instructed to report to our respective sports grounds for the upcoming military recruitment drive. This development presented a new challenge for me, as I realized I lacked the necessary documentation for military recruitment. My certificates were still in the possession of my uncle in Nairobi, who claimed to have returned them to me on a previous occasion, which was untrue. Without my certificates, my prospects for military recruitment appeared bleak.

Despite my predicament, I remained determined to pursue alternative avenues for employment. Hearing rumors of a sports recruitment drive at Langata military base, I seized the opportunity and participated in a five-thousand-meter race, finishing within the top five. As one of the twenty selected candidates, I eagerly awaited further instructions, hopeful that this opportunity would provide a pathway to my desired career path. I participated in 5,000 meters finishing 5th with unofficial 14.56. All that was important was position and finishing top 10 in every heat was good indicator; there were about ten 500 meters heats,

However, my aspirations were dashed when the recruitment process abruptly ended. A military helicopter landed on the track, ushering in a group of young men accompanied by military personnel. Over the course of several hours, candidates were called one by one, leaving the remaining hopefuls in a state of uncertainty. With the recruitment process abruptly terminated and no explanation provided, I realized that my ambitions of joining the military had been indefinitely postponed.

Discontent with my current circumstances, I was fueled by a burning determination to surpass my limitations and vowed to myself that I was far from finished. Despite the setbacks I encountered, I resolved to give it another try, firmly believing that success was still within reach. Returning home with a wealth of skills acquired during my time with the military, along with a newfound sense of stealth and focus, I was determined to elevate my training regimen to new heights.

Seeking guidance and structure in my pursuit of excellence, I approached a man named Silvan Mwangile, who had obtained his coaching certification after abandoning his running career due to an injury one year earlier. Recognizing his desire for coaching although he had no history in coaching, I sought to make him my training guide just to avoid training without anyone observing my mechanic. I was the first person he tested his coaching skills if they were optimal or not; any bad guidance would be reflective of his knowledge in coaching., I didn't care at the moment. I was ready to take the risk but I had to use my own discernment on any prescription whatsoever. I requested him to devise the most rigorous training program he could conceive. Drawing upon my experiences in the military, where I had tested my limits and acquired invaluable knowledge, I was very confident he didn't understand my abilities so whatever he could prescribe was within my body functions. All I sought was systematic and organized approach to my training.

With Silvan's assistance, I embarked on a training regimen designed to push me beyond my perceived boundaries and propel me towards my goals. Each day became an opportunity to challenge myself physically and mentally, as I embraced every intensity of the workouts and remained steadfast in my commitment to improvement.

As I immersed myself in the demanding program, I knew that every step I took brought me closer to realizing my aspirations and fulfilling my potential. However, the public did not see things my way; their own lenses that portrayed insanity of a destitute child, the perception was that I was riding on a dying horse that will cripple over time. Others devalued my effort to appoint of blatant abuse. I recall one day I brought a bottle of drinking water and placed it at the soccer goal post.

There was a team of volleyball players from Kenya Post Office practicing at the same time. It happened that as I circled on track one man ran to my water and drank all of it. To me I didn't see him drink the water but I saw him running back to his playing position coming from the direction where I had placed my water bottle, but I didn't suspect anything. It was until I needed the water, I realized my water was gone. Later on upon being confronted about his actions, his response was that "I don't care, his running will never take him anywhere". These were basic challenges that occurred here and there. Other times drivers had no reason to slow down for me as I ran on the dusty roads. I remember matatu drivers will blanket me with cloud of dust while you are streaming sweat. By the time you return home from a long run, a sticky brown lava flows down your body from this gust of dust mixed with your sweat.

Silvans training program consisted of three main components: morning runs, midday runs, and evening jogs. With unwavering dedication, I faithfully adhered to this structured regimen for four months under his guidance. His presence during the workouts served as both motivation and accountability, forging a deep bond between us as he assumed the role of both friend and coach. As the new season approached, I felt prepared and eager to put my training to the test.

That following year 1993, I set my own goal and an ultimatum. The goal was to try one more notch above what I had done previous years; if there is no success by the end of the year I would quit running, look for a life partner and delve in regular life just like everyone else in the village. The first event of the season took place not far from my hometown, and I arrived at the venue punctually after a morning journey. Competing in the senior men's twelve-kilometer cross country race, I surprised myself by finishing in sixth place in time of thirty-eight minutes; feat that garnered attention when my name appeared in the sports section of the national newspaper the following day. I was excited with my name featured throughout radio stations and television broadcasts, sparking excitement and curiosity among many.

Emboldened by my success, I intensified my training regimen while maintaining the same pattern established by Silvania. As the second event approached, held at JUCAT (Kenyatta university), I found myself faced with a new challenge. Dan, who everyone looked upon for mentorship, decided to change my event to the 20-kilometer road race. Despite the grueling nature of the race; my first time running on tarmac and covering such a distance; I pushed myself to the limit and crossed the finish line in an impressive eighth position in unofficial time of one hours and 6 seconds. Once again, my achievements garnered attention from various news media outlets, further solidifying my determination to pursue my athletic goals with unwavering focus.

At this point I decided to secretly increase my training without letting Silvan know my threshold; my daily morning run was sixteen kilometers on a very hilly terrain to be completed by eight in the morning. I would rest for two hours and job to Moi Stadium Embu where I will meet a contingent of runners with volunteering coaches. I would conceal my earlier training and join them for whatever training they were subjected to. Later I would go home jogging again for lunch and rest. I would later get out for un specified jog depending on my energy levels.

During that season, my road performance showcased a remarkable consistency, as I finished all races within the top ten. My prowess on the road became a sensation, and my competitors feared my entry into any road race. However, despite my success on the track, poverty continued to cast its shadow over my family.

An unforgettable incident unfolded before a crucial meeting in Nyahururu. Lacking the funds to travel and register for the event, I faced a potential setback. Dan, my mentor, left a message in Embu, urging me to find a way to Nyahururu, assuring me that he would cover my return journey and accommodation. Determined to participate, I worked tirelessly that week in a neighbor's farm, harvesting corn during the day and squeezing in evening training sessions.

In the weeks leading up to the event, I contacted my uncle, a resident of town of Nyahururu where the event was to be held; he graciously agreed to host me for the night before the cross-country race, coincidentally he rented less than a kilometer from the cross country venue. We coordinated the details and set a time to meet before he left town. Armed with a little more than enough fare, I traveled to Nyahururu with the assurance of a place to sleep for the night and the promise of return bus fare from Dan.

Upon my arrival at around 3:00 pm, my uncle was nowhere to be found. In a moment of uncertainty, I roamed the town, contemplating his potential locations, including his office at the County Council offices. Unable to locate him, I decided to head to the cross-country venue. There, I found Dan engrossed in marking the field. He welcomed me with joy and instructed me to wait while he completed his tasks. However, in the midst of his duties, Dan unintentionally forgot about my presence, and I watched as he left the venue in a police Land Rover, driving away from the opposite side of the field.

Unsure where to trace Dan in town, I scoured the streets without luck, checking on every possible den, pub, lodge and hotels. I had no choice but to find a meal that would fuel my body for the challenges ahead. With limited resources at my disposal, I carefully weighed my options before finally securing a modest meal within my budget. Satisfied with my meager purchase, I retraced my steps to my uncle's residence which was less that a kilometer to the cross-country meeting venue, hoping for a change of fortune upon my return.

As I reached my uncle's doorstep, anticipation mingled with apprehension. Sitting in wait until the late hours of the night, I harbored a glimmer of hope that he might return and offer shelter for the night. However, as the minutes ticked by without any sign of his presence, I realized that my prospects were dwindling.

Turning to a neighbor for assistance, I divulged my predicament, laying bare the challenges I faced. Sympathetic to my plight, the neighbor said he have just received guests who will share his only available guest rooms; he extended an offer of refuge, albeit in the humble surroundings of his milking shed. Grateful for his generosity, I accepted his offer, preparing to spend the night under the starlit sky, armed with nothing but a few makeshift comforts to ward off the encroaching darkness.

With the dawn of a new day, I found myself at the race venue, eager to face the challenges ahead despite the absence of breakfast and the chill of the morning air. As I arrived, I encountered a few fellow runners who had arrived early to familiarize themselves with the route before the competition commenced, their footsteps echoing as they jogged back to their respective hotels for preparation to run.

Undeterred by the circumstances, I prepared myself mentally for the grueling twenty-five-kilometer distance that lay ahead. As the race unfolded, I pushed myself to the limits, determined to leave everything on the track. However, as I approached the 22-kilometer mark, fatigue threatened to overwhelm me, and for a fleeting moment, I teetered on the brink of surrender.

Yet, just when I felt my strength waning, a surge of encouragement washed over me as the military contingent who knew me from the time the previous year when I was under their training command rallied around me and my performance; their cheers igniting a fire within me. Fueled by their unwavering support, adrenaline power erupted within, I summoned every ounce of determination pushing through the pain barrier with a newfound resolve.

In the end, I crossed the finish line in second place in one hour 19 minutes, my body weary but my spirit triumphant. Despite the dizzying challenges I faced along the way, the unwavering support of my comrades-in-arms propelled me forward, serving as a testament to the indomitable spirit that resides within us all.

Despite the lack of immediate support from Dan, my determination remained unwavering as I continued to pursue my passion for running.

Fortunately, after the event fate smiled upon me when I was offered a ride back to Embu by the Kenya Prison team, who had come to participate in the cross-country event. Their generosity provided me with a means to return home and continue my journey.

****

Every year I saw new comers who come with high expectations and will fade away as fast as they arrive; I noticed older runners missing every year and never to ever come back as they pursue other endeavors. It was a common statement at every end of the season people saying goodbye to one another with one common statement, "Your efforts will make us meet again". I would ask myself every time if my efforts were to the standard to enable me to meet the same competitive friends. It was a self-assessment that made me keep my running to bar.

The cross-country season was up again which acted and the build up events for the entire running year. Charles trained with me as well as others who were new or long-time runners. That year provincial cross-country championship was in town of Machakos. Our training involved a series of intervals, fartlek and hill sprints. However, my body had banked enough training far beyond the cross country distance. We arrived the night before and stayed with Charles in the same hotel room. We warmed up as team and lined up for the race. It was twelve-kilometer race running from Kenyatta stadium crossing through the shops running up the toward Machakos hills then the route diverting toward the residential area that led down the valley. With minimal markings on the route, there was a marks man at every intersection who would direct us which way to follow.

At eight kilometers mark Embu team was leading with a huge gap. Charles was running next to me in a park of five runners. The marks man pointed to us the wrong direction which we followed down to the stream where we come to a stop at the water. We found ourselves convincingly crossing the stream and continuing running. We couldn't find the route back to the stadium. We stopped and walked, talking to villagers seeking the way back to the stadium.

As we jogged back to the stadium, we were amazed to see every one seated and awards was underway; about ten of us, eight runners from Embu and two others from Kitui were intentionally re-routed to the wrong direction. They had already named the team to represent the province. With protest we pushed to know how and why we were rerouted to the wrong direction intentionally while those runners from Machakos knew the plot to misdirect non residence runners. The team to represent Eastern province was recompiled with inclusion of the misrouted runners to save the officials from public wrath. At the national championships none of the favored runners from the cheat town finished top forty.

Despite these challenges, my advancement continued in my favor. I found myself thrust into the realm of the Kenyan police athletics team, a fortuitous opportunity that presented itself when they required swift runners to accompany their training sessions. As the designated pacers for various distances and especially speed work, we enjoyed the perks of complimentary meals and transportation to various events. While some individuals relied on patronage to secure a spot within the police force, such avenues were not accessible to me. My family's impoverished circumstances meant that we lacked the means to grease the wheels of bribery. Faced with this reality, I resolved to navigate the challenges through sheer determination and unwavering faith in a higher power.

Charles Gitau was impressed by my performance, extended a heartfelt gesture of support by promising a monthly donation to cover half a liter of milk every day. This act of kindness sustained me for three months, providing much-needed nourishment as I intensified my training regimen in preparation for upcoming events.

As summer approached, I seized the opportunity to showcase my skills in the Military twenty-one-kilometer race, where I delivered an impressive performance, finishing second with a time of one hour and two minutes. This was my first paid earnings from a race with some form of cash. My dedication and perseverance were beginning to yield tangible results, propelling me closer to my goals with each stride.

Every year I evaluated my years performance and achievements. Everyone from my training group admired my achievements and changed my projection. I was in the right path and as cross-country season was nearing, I continued with my training occasionally meeting Dan whenever he was in town

***

1994 was the transitional year between my amateur status and entry to professional running in my career. The cycle of cross country was back, from district to the nationals. I won the Embu District Cross country Championships and third at the provincial level headed to Nationals, I stamped an assurance of performance to the previous favored runners from cheating town where we were intentionally misrouted. At the Nationals I finished thirty-eight; I was the best rated road runners in the country for my consistency and best runner from my province earning myself a position at the national team. I was included in the Kenyan marathon team destined for residential camp.

KAAA had made a decision to set a residential training camp for marathoners together at the cross-country team at St. Marks Teachers College in Embu. I was among the fourteen selected for this rigorous training.

The training was rigorous and everyday become a competition among ourselves. After one week I suffered a knee injury. It was so painful that I would trail behind due to excruciating pain. The most humiliating part was that we were in my home district where almost everyone knew me; I felt ashamed as people who knew me calling my name while trailing behind this National contingent limping. I went to see Dan on the third day of my injury. He asked me what the hell was going on with me and if I want to shame him and my community after making it all the way to National team, then here behaving incompetent. To Dan pain was not an excuse; you got to be strong minded and wear a lion heart! He gave me two options; pack my things and leave or play with the rules or the game. In his own words Dan said to me, "There is a litany of athletes who would love to be in your position, you can mess as much as you want there is no exception, you are in the National team, here we don't baby feed anyone, if you want you can leave just now!" What followed was concealing feelings on pain, no pain no gain analogy. That weekend Dan introduced some training never done before. Three hours long run was to be to executed without exception. There was a bus trailing us in case one faints and there was adequate fluids, fruits and team doctor was on board. From St. marks Teachers College, we boarded the college bus at three o'clock in the afternoon headed 25 Km south of Embu town a place called Gatondo Village which is low attitude compared to where we will finish the run at the end of Mt. kenya. Training started four 0'clock passing through Embu Town suburbs.

The first water station was at Kangaru Secondary School after forty minutes. There after we headed through Kangaru village. With my painful injuries at that point, I faded; the College bus which was following us was out of sight.

The next water station was after one hour at Kairuri market. By the time I arrived at Kairuri Market I had run for one hour twenty-five minutes. I relied on by standers asking them which route did the running group follow. The bus would stop at designated spots for water; I missed the next two water stops as the coaches had instructed the driver on how long to stay at one spot as well as not to carry anyone unless they appeared sick. I arrived at the end of Mt. Kenya Forest in two hours and change. At the edge of Mt. Kenya I saw the college bus where Dan with three runners whom appeared exhausted. I took water, Dan pointed to me the path into the forest direction asking me to keep on. For some reason I was happy that I was not the first one to drop though I was in pain.

It was turning dark and the forest canopy added some ambiguity in the run. Running alone, I continued another fifteen minutes. All of a sudden I met poachers with over fifty dogs. The dogs were well mannered and under control. I was in a shock as I had never seen such a group of dogs. About four men were carrying heavy bags while surrounded and commanded the this army of dogs. I spoke Kiembu to them asking them to protect me from the dogs and if they have seen some runners. They said they are about three minutes up the forest.

The intricate fearful moment, the immense shock while my muscles were ward and fragile and abrupt muscle twitch from this scenc in time; all these occurrences did magic in me. The pain and injury disappeared instantly.

I found myself freely moving with ease; as I ran, I wasn't sure if it was myself again. It was surreal! Another 35 minutes into the forest loop brought be to the edge of the forest. It was already dark. The remaining distance was along the edge to the forest heading back to where the bus was packed. I caught up with five runners who half ran and half walked. As I passed them, I gained more strength; by the time I arrived at the bus I had run for three hours and ten minutes. The moment I got in the bus, Dan looked at me smiling and said, "You are one lucky man, bus was leaving in five minutes"

Inside the bus I saw only six runners from the team of fourteen athletes. After five minutes the bus started moving leaving the rest of the of the runners to find their way to St, Marks, another fifteen kilometers in the night.

The miraculous three hour training that transformed and reconfigured my injuries into perfect athlete. From that day onwards, I joined the ranks of those prospects of prime events abroad. Dan Muchoki gained much more confident in me and was always ready to advocate for my inclusion in the National team.

That training saw my first international appearance; my name was in the list of invited runners where by I was slated to run in Humburg Marathon.

In another change of events, my involvement with the Kenyan police team proved to be instrumental in shaping my athletic journey. From 1995 onward, I was consistently privileged to be at residential training sessions at St. Mark Kigari Teachers College for cross country events. Additionally, we convened at Embu hotels during the track and field seasons, where the team gathered for meals. Our participation extended to all their regional events, marking a period of significant immersion within their athletic circle.

However, this affiliation also introduced a divide within my local community. As my ties with the Kenyan police strengthened, a gap emerged in my local friendships. I tried to influence younger runners to join me but they appeared skeptical and didn't believe that I am normal individual. Some villagers grew wary of my continuous association with police force, harboring suspicions that I might be acting as a clandestine informant for the authorities. This apprehension stemmed from fears that my allegiance to the police team could potentially compromise their unconventional lifestyles, leading to distrust and alienation within the community. To me losing one or two confidants in the community replacing them with more knowledgeable friend from the wider sporting network significantly improving my career wasn't of any concerns.

Consequently, this self-instill fear from my fellow villagers hindered their gain and benefit from me as exemplary role model. This is a fact that didn't great my conscious.

Following this, I realized I can only coach my younger brother to join in this crime of running and gain exponentially from my connections in sports.

***

Amidst my athletic endeavors, an unexpected opportunity arose when the Kenya Amateur Athletics Association (KAAA) offered myself and Joseph Kahugu the chance to participate in a student exchange program in Korea. This invitation opened new doors for personal and athletic growth, presenting an exciting chapter in my journey as a runner.

The reality of our situation in Korea diverged sharply from the expectations we had harbored. Instead of enrolling in language studies at Seoul University as initially conveyed, Joseph and I found ourselves under the care of a Korean coach in Taegu City, located in the Youngcheon Province. Our days were soon filled with grueling training sessions that surpassed even the rigors of military training I had endured previously.

We stayed in a standard hotel but with no conventional bed; we slept on Korean Style setting though that appeared very strange to me. The floors are heated; a soft mart representing a bed and two very heavy duvet, one to spread down and the second one to cover yourself. There was no television, kitchen and no phones, it was just a plain sleeping quarter.

The initial two weeks of our stay in Korea were characterized by the biting chill of snowy mornings and freezing temperatures, a harsh environment to which we were unaccustomed, especially considering it was our first encounter with temperatures below 15 degrees Celsius. Despite the physical discomfort, what struck us was the abundance of food provided to sustain us through our rigorous training regimen. However, this generosity was tempered by careful monitoring to prevent overeating and maintain our nutritional balance.

Each morning, for the first two weeks of our stay, we arose at the unforgiving hour of four in the morning. Our coach would then lead us on a one-hour drive to a nearby golf club, where we embarked on our training regimen before the course maintenance team arrived. This routine saw us running for a staggering two hours every day; a stark departure from our accustomed training sessions, which had never exceeded such lengths except during marathon competitions. He introduced a novel training approach involving track-based long runs, a departure from our usual routines. On days when we didn't head to the golf course, he would transport us to the track, pacing us from behind in his car as we embarked on grueling twenty-one-kilometer runs. With a megaphone mounted on his vehicle, he would shout instructions and encouragement to us throughout the session. The golf management sooner noticed our footsteps on icy grass and decided on day to come early. We were confronted and a stern warning was issued to our coach. That was the end of our golf course training however the 4 am waking up never stopped, this time it was track running. Our coached chased us behind with his car on the track.

However, this unconventional method of training carried significant risks. The proximity of the car meant that we had to maintain precise control over our movements to avoid potential accidents. Any misstep could result in serious injury or a run over, especially considering the high speeds at which we were running. Unfortunately, I fell again into my customed habits whenever my training regimen is altered; I suffered yet another injury. This time a severe knee injury during one of these sessions.

Despite the coach's innovative approach and dedication to our improvement, the inherent dangers of this training regimen became apparent. The pursuit of athletic excellence often comes with sacrifices, but it's crucial to prioritize safety and well-being. The intensity of our training in Korea pushed us beyond our limits, both physically and mentally.

Enduring the predawn hours and the relentless demands placed upon us, Joseph and I found ourselves tested in ways we had never imagined. Yet, amidst the exhaustion and challenges, there was a sense of determination; a steadfast resolve to persevere and extract every ounce of potential from within ourselves.

Each day, as we braced ourselves against the cold, our breakfast consisted of a modest portion of a small packet of milk—a meager yet essential start to fuel our bodies for the demanding day ahead. For lunch, we were served a humble hamburger devoid of any meat patty, containing only salad—a simple fare that emphasized sustenance over extravagance. Similarly, he made sure we don't eat as much to keep our weights low, our dinners comprised approximately a piece of roasted pork accompanied by salad, not which was too little to replenish our energy reserves after the day's exertions.

Despite the stringent dietary regimen and the harsh climate, we persevered, driven by the shared determination to excel in our training and represent our country with distinction. Each meal became a vital source of nourishment therefore in order to sustain ourselves we would bravely jump over the window to escape his watch which he sometimes did by staying a little longer in the hallway to listen and monitor us. One of us would jump out and buy bread and soda to maintain our nutritional energies in pursuit of our athletic aspirations. I couldn't shake the feeling that our health was beginning to deteriorate. The physical toll of our rigorous regimen was evident as we gradually became underweight, our bodies displaying signs of strain and exhaustion.

Personally, I noticed a concerning development; I experienced an empty pouch forming in my stomach, a consequence of the abrupt transition from consuming substantial amounts of food to subsisting on meager rations, such as a single burger.

Moreover, I began experiencing persistent hiccups, particularly after drinking water. Initially dismissed as a minor inconvenience, but this issue soon escalated, becoming increasingly frequent and disruptive. It reached a point where the simple act of hydrating triggered relentless bouts of hiccups, disrupting my daily routines and causing considerable discomfort. To my dismay, this problem intensified further to point I could smell water from a tap or a container for an additional four years, casting a shadow over my overall well-being and raising concerns about the long-term effects of our demanding training regimen.

Towards the end of the second week, distressing news reached us: our manager and coach had been involved in a horrific road accident, leaving his Daewoo car mangled wreckage. He suffered severe injuries, including the need for open brain surgery, and was hospitalized for an extended period. In his absence, we found ourselves under the guidance of a new coach, whose approach was notably less intense.

However, just two week after his accident, an unexpected visitor arrived one night, knocking on our door; it was around 11 pm. To our astonishment, it was our hospitalized coach, discreetly concealing his intravenous drips beneath his jacket. Despite his precarious condition, he expressed a fervent desire to oversee our training, determined not to let his injuries impede his involvement in our athletic pursuits. This clandestine arrangement persisted for another two weeks until he was finally discharged from the hospital and able to rejoin us for training sessions.

Upon his return, our coach exhibited a renewed sense of determination, intensifying our training regimen with a vengeance. As the demands grew more arduous, I found myself grappling with injuries and a growing desire to return home was inevitable. Despite the coach's unwavering commitment and dedication to our development, the physical toll on my body left me contemplating my future in the sport.

Despite the setback of my injuries, they inadvertently provided a temporary reprieve, as my training partner Joseph diligently completed all the prescribed training sessions. Meanwhile, I found myself gravitating toward the treadmill for most of my workouts, coupled with regular ultrasound treatments at a nearby hospital.

However, this routine took an unexpected turn when I sustained a skin burn during one of my treatments, unbeknownst to me until a sudden, sharp itching sensation alerted me to the damage. Upon attempting to alleviate the discomfort by scratching, my skin peeled away, leaving behind an open wound.

***

In the days that followed, I opted to train away from the prying eyes of my coach and Joseph who were engrossed in the usual rigorous track sessions. Seeking solace in a bush near the stadium, I discovered a slight incline that proved conducive to my rehabilitation effort; a gentle gradient that allowed for a half-hour jog every session. Astonishingly, by the following few days my knee injury had miraculously subsided, prompting a surge of jubilation. This injury had lingered for nearly six weeks, causing considerable frustration and doubt about my athletic pursuits. I eagerly continued training privately for fear of returning full time to Josephs training dosage.

Despite my injury woes, our manager delivered unexpected news: Joseph and I were to compete at Teagu marathon in three weeks time. This sudden opportunity served as both a source of motivation and apprehension, propelling us into a heightened state of preparation as we braced ourselves for the challenges that lay ahead on the marathon course.

At this juncture, our coach cum manager seemed unconvinced of my ability to deliver commendable results, given my injury sidelining me for a month and a half, especially in contrast to Joseph's rigorous training regimen. Therefore, he concerted his time and focus to Joseph compounding his training. Despite the mounting pressure, I personally felt a sense of urgency to regain my health and leave this situation behind. We repeatedly inquired about the commencement of the language school at the university as promised earlier, only to realize that our hopes for it were unfounded. I was aware that we are not going to enroll in any school and there was some form of deceit on the agreement that sailed us through which was signed my KAAA.

The race day was here where we entered among various international athletes. The marathon started and ended at the same track that was well maintained with tartan different from where we did our training. Our usual training track was gravel.

I didn't know how events unfolded but I remember lining up for the marathon. I started slow because I was aware of my potential drop due to my injury, paced myself incrementally. Joseph was ready to perform and my expectation was he will do well at least because he didn't halt his training the entire time. At fifteen kilometers I caught up few Kenyans including Joseph who said he was experiencing some pain. At twenty one kilometers I was still unsure of what will happen with my less painful injury. I moved on and at thirty-eight kilometers I realized I was still strong and tried accelerating more toward the end. I finished eighth overall. I slashed six minutes out of my personal best to two hours and twelve minutes automatically qualifying for the Olympics. It was a glorious moment for me to finish a marathon with so little training. What I learned was that you can't lose your fitness in one month especially with the training involved in marathons. As for my coach manager he was amazed and surprised by my performance against his expectation. We attended the award ceremony with great resistance, we knew at every race there is an award ceremony where the winners get their winnings. Though everything was in Korean language we had met with some American agents at the race who had told us about the banquet at the host hotel the same night. We asked our coach manager about the banquet and he said it was not important. He said we need to rest for the following days training. Joseph and I insisted we need to go and join everyone else and it was our only chance to meet with fellow Kenyans since we don't see any black person around us. With low opinion he accepted and realized we are aware of the procedures surrounding marathon events. The dinner was great and I was awarded my winning which was a certificate and instructions how to get the money. The winning was eight million Korea money and equivalent of six thousand US dollars. What broke my heart was that my winning was divided into three portions: Coach manager, Joseph and myself. Joseph and myself got equal amount. This was devastating to me and I felt used. I resisted and the coach manager said according to Korean sporting rules, every winning belongs to the team and its shared equally. I lost interest of being there following the unfolding of events.

Joseph finished with injuries he had to take several days off from training to recover.

In my case, the second day after the marathon, the coach manager took us to the same track where the marathon started; told me the days workout was 21 repeats of a thousand meters. I told him that we need to reduce our training the week following the marathon to allow the body regain the and rebuild for further intensive training. He insisted that this is normal in Korea and need to be done, where I was made to do one-kilometer intervals twenty-one repeats. Reluctantly I did the training and when I finished my whole body was numb and felt every bone in my body as if its separating from the fresh.

The training went on as if I didn't run a marathon; I continued to get weaker and frail. We made friends who would sneak food to our apartment when our coach manager was away. Our coach cum manager discovered that we are getting food from friends. He would therefore come to our room and throw all the foods away. It became apparent that he recorded anything that we ate, amount of rest, amount of water we drink though he didn't sleep in the same apartment.

The third week after the marathon I made my decision to leave and leave Joseph behind; therefore I asked the coach manager to book my return flight to Nairobi Kenya. I called KAAA to inform them the odious treatment we are undergoing, similarly I called my mother to inform her I am on my way home and I can't continue with thus torturous training. No one knew what we were going through and advises weren't to the degree of our suffering.

Joseph wasn't as open and clear to what he wanted however he knew life would not be easier for him alone. He pleaded with me not to leave him behind because he doesn't know how he can make it alone. I gave him my stance and he joined my call to leave. Our flights were booked and we were on our way to the airport. At the airport the coach manager pleaded to us asking if we can change our minds last minute for some form of agreement. We declined and he saw us off shedding tears ; it was too late for me. Joseph was free to turn back but he didn't. We left Korea in a taste of uncertainty if we would return or not. In Nairobi we had to write a report on why we choose to cancel the exchange program so early. It was at that time we explained Athletics Kenya that we discovered the deal wasn't about language school, it was sports brokerage scheme, with their approval on without their knowledge, it was a hoax. It was rumored that three years later the same coach cum manager received two other Kenyan runners who lived a little different. Unlike us who lived in Korean Style setting though it was hotel standard the new entrants now had conventional bed, television, microwave and table phone. Words come across that after the marathon, the coach manager took the two men back to the hotel, drugged the two men through drinks and pretended to leave them to rest. While the drugs took then into deep sleep, he later come back and entered the apartment, handcuffed them on bed and put the phone far away from them and left for the evening banquet. He came later at midnight to find the Kenyans had woken up and somehow alerted the police of the mischief. Following this mischievous act the two athletes launched police complain which landed the coach manager a three months jail time in Korea.

What I had acquired in Korean trip was mental training skill though I paid heavily for that acquisition, I leaped a lot there after.

Back in Embu, I was now ready to put my combined knowledge in practice; The self-driven ambitions combined with the military training skill, refined with the Korean mental training. In addition, my body had undergone a litany of illness that hardened my soul and instilled unbreakable spirit to thrive. I knew no one had undergone the kind of life testing like myself. I compared my body to a machine made from tested material that can withstand rigorous training. I was aware of the machine in me that just need servicing. I had training materials to move me to the next level but I want sure how soon that will happen.

***

Before my next move I knew that my success will now depend on my food security and transportation and I had addressed that with caution.

With much of the knowledge surrounding training my goal was to run twenty kilometers everyday which may come in different forms, either one full session or two split session and sometime three session as long as the combined mileages added to twenty kilometers. I made sure I recorded every bit of my training. The same year I won Eastern Province cross country stunningly defeating the well-known top runners from province. The shockwave was national wide which led to an invitation to Beijing Marathon the same year.

Now I had a target race which later one become my signature event. I structured my training focused on shuttering all records on every route I used to run. I set my own goals and standard based on what others were doing. Several days I secretly did more than my coach advised me to avoid open challenge among my peers. It became evident that whatever me and my coach will attempt as new strategy he would then go and prescribe the same to my competitors of which they would in turn try to outrun me. That made me standout to my peers and they handily understood my training technics. Following my return to Beijing marathon same year, I shed off three minutes from my previous two hours and sixteen minutes on the same course as I finished fourth. The results were again published and broadcasted national wide sending a wave of excitement in running circles.

Jubilant and joy in my family for staining a mark of recognition in the world of sport and also a prospective candidate for international stage. It was now clear that I am a full-time athlete requiring vigorous and extra ordinary disciplines to move the next stage. The following season running from October cross country was the main focus. What followed was a world class documentary with National Geographic television, an exercise that delved in the intracity of kenyans success in the world of athletics. The documentary "Kenya Crandle of Champions" features Paul Tergat and myself. The scenes of the video include Kigali Teacher training college where the Kenyan Cross Country team camped every year, my parent's home, all my routes and the Kenya Police team as my training partners. It was a breakthrough moment for me. That inclusion motivated me and the same year I was included in the Kenyan marathoner's team to train at Kapsabet under Ibrahim Hussein. Dan Muchoki declined to join the training camp even as the national head Coach, in fact he tried to walk me out of joining that residential camp citing the tribal nature of those involved. Just as Dan had predicted, unfortunately, there was much hype among the administration and the coaches toward selecting team members for Boston marathon, Paris marathon, Rotterdam and London marathon that requested from marathon runners through Kim McDonalds. Many of the prospectives were left out and replaced with young runners from Rift Valley alluding that we were not fit for the events. This was the first time the tribal card got live in my presence. While we were busy an undercurrent was going on; it was apparent that several runners and coaches from Kenya were writing letters directly to Beijing marathon organizers stating that they were in greater shape than myself. Unaware of this undercurrent, David Okeyo who was neither a Kisii, Kalenjin nor kikuyu or Kamba the four top tribe that competed in top performances called me to his office and told me that Beijing marathon has sent a letter of invitation specifically requesting my participation. A glare of hope shown in my heart followed by intensive training. As I sank into deep training in Embu, a lot of athletes kept of sending false statements about my fitness hoping they could replace me. Luckily Dan Muchoki who was always in Nairobi updated me on all these claims urging me to keep focused.

That year I participated in fifteen hundred meters at district competition finishing second in three minutes and fifty-five seconds; moved to five thousand meters in fourteen-thirty-eight and ten thousand meters in twenty-eight minutes and twenty-eight seconds at provincial level.

Athletics administrators from Eastern province which had their headquarters in Embu demonstrated bizarre behavior, scheming to hide funds meant for taking the provincial team to the national Championships in Nairobi.

It became apparent that there was always a chaotic situation with the Eastern Province teams preparation to the national championships. After assembling at Embu Stadium and waiting for several hours, it became evident that something was amiss. The promised funds for the provincial team to travel to the national Championships in Nairobi weren't available; no money to pay for bus to take runners to the national championships in Nairobi despite funds being sent out from KAAA headquarters a week prior. Athletes, coaches, and supporters grew increasingly frustrated as the delay stretched on without any explanation from the administrators. It was a disheartening experience for everyone involved, especially considering the hard work and dedication the athletes had put into their training.

Finally, a mini bus pulled up, it was hired to transport us to Nairobi; arriving just minutes before the KAAA office closes for athletes' registration. After Athlete registration, the bus proceeded to Kenya Science Teacher College hostels awaiting the three days event at Kasarani. The Mini-bus dropped us and left.

At the national championship I ran only ten thousand meters where I finished 13th in 29.13. This helped me achieve and maintain speed at a particular plateau for next race. However, the challenges didn't end there. The day after the championships, we faced another ordeal: most officials had left directly from Kasarani Sports ground to their homes, abandoning the team. It seemed they were aware that there were no funds available to transport the runners back to Embu. Left stranded at the Kenya Science Teacher College hostel, we waited for eight hours as hunger began to set in among the athletes. It was ironic that the same runners who had represented their province with pride were now asked to contribute whatever they could afford to raise money for a minibus so that we could return home.

Upon our return to Embu, we were greeted with mixed emotions. While there was relief to be back home after the tumultuous experience, there was also a lingering sense of disappointment and frustration with the athletics administrators who had failed to fulfill their responsibilities. Many of us felt let down by the system that was meant to support and nurture our athletic talents.

However, amidst the challenges and setbacks, our love for running remained unwavering. We were determined to overcome obstacles and continue pursuing our passion for athletics. This experience served as a reminder of the resilience and determination ingrained within us as athletes, driving us to push forward despite the obstacles in our path.

In October I was on my way to Beijing marathon. On arrival as usual many runners got appearance monies but this time, I was challenged by the Chinese athletics association to proof my fitness on the race and only when I finish in top five, I will get my appearance fee. They alluded to some emails and faxes sent from Kenya that I have not been training effectively. They claimed that several Kenyan Coaches and runners had sent a litany of reports seeking my replacement citing that I am busy with my computer business and not training. I was tasked to proof my shape and fitness on the race. On the race day I knew chances of walking back home with nothing but few gifts we had received as a team were high. Any stupid mistake would render me penniless. We lined up against Tanzanians, Ethiopians, Zimbabweans, Belarussians, Hungary, Koreans and the host Chinese. I started slow and increased as we advanced in distances. Oblivious to who was leading, at fifteen kilometers I noticed the pace in my group was slow and decided to push the pace a little higher. This late acceleration saw us crossing half mark with one hour and two minutes. Abebe Makonnen who had a lot of experience lead our second pack and started some fartlek racing tactic for another five-kilometer breaking up the sizeable pack. Around thirty kilometers only four of us were left in our group, two Ethiopians and a Chinese. Unaware to me, one Belarusian athlete took off with the half-marathon competitors and was running alone after 21 kilometers. By thirty-five kilometers we caught up with this man who paced himself and left everyone behind. He was running in a constant pace and our advancement meant nothing other than rendering him as non-challenger. He did not pose any threat whatsoever as we disappeared on the horizon. I finished first with two hours, ten minutes and thirty-eight minutes.

***

From that pivotal moment, I underwent a profound transformation. I forged new connections while bidding farewell to old friends, a transition that left me in a state of profound disbelief. Yet, amidst this upheaval, my passion for running only intensified. The tangible rewards of my dedication to the sport began to materialize in various facets of my life. My family, now fully cognizant of my burgeoning potential, witnessed firsthand the trajectory of my success.

Emboldened by my newfound sense of purpose, I ventured beyond the confines of our family's land, acquiring property of my own.

That same year I was named as one of Kenyan marathon runners to participate in Olympics in Atlanta USA. I did my training at Nairobi national residential camp after luckily presenting my province in 10,000 m race. I was the last one with 28 minutes and some change; a lap behind William Sigei's 27 minutes and change. While waiting for the final team to the

Olympics, I was disheartened to find my name replace with Lameck Aguta in the marathon team because he was training in USA. Somehow the officials considered saving travel cost and pickup someone near the Olympic venue. It was heart breaking especially when no one gave reasons for dropping my name from the list. Sub 29 in in track for a marathon runner was great timing at the time.

"You are dump if you do and dump when you do!" I was the only Marathon runner who participated at the National track and field finals yet I was left out from the Atlanta Olympics despite being short listed.

Following my rising profile, I found myself inundated with invitations from international sports agents, each vying to represent me in various competitions across the globe. After careful consideration, I selected an American agent to serve as my representative, entrusting them with the task of securing opportunities for me in the USA. Under their guidance, I embarked on a journey that led me to participate in prestigious events such as the Boston Marathon, along with numerous local races, over the course of a year.

Simultaneously, amidst my athletic pursuits, I began to cultivate a newfound interest in computer studies. Recognizing the importance of diversifying my skill set, my agent facilitated introductory lessons in computer programming and software applications. This exposure ignited a passion within me for the world of technology, prompting me to delve deeper into the realm of computers and digital literacy.

However, our collaboration eventually soured due to disagreements over financial matters. It came to light that the agent had made substantial withdrawals from my bank account without my consent, exploiting a loophole that allowed them full authority over athlete funds. The manager, in a shrewd move, had ensured that every athlete under their purview designated the agent as a co-signer or granted them unrestricted access to their accounts in their absence.

Despite the agent's justification that the funds were earmarked for the purchase of a new residence to be utilized by athletes, suspicions arose regarding the exorbitant amounts withdrawn. Questions lingered about the transparency and integrity of the financial transactions, casting a shadow of doubt over the agent's motives and prompting a reevaluation of our professional relationship. Expressing my grievances to the agent, I underscored the financial strain I was enduring during my time in the United States. Despite my efforts, I lamented that I had not been able to generate any income, as all the appearance fees I had earned were swiftly depleted by the exorbitant one-year rent, which was deducted whether I stayed for a week or a month. Compounding my frustration was the unjust deduction of a pre-race commission of 15%, extracted from the anticipated winnings of the pending Beijing Marathon, months before the actual event in October.

Overwhelmed by a sense of indignation and betrayal, I reached a breaking point, realizing that continuing under the terms of this contract was untenable. The sheer injustice of these financial arrangements left me incensed, compelling me to sever ties with the agent once and for all. With no prospect of financial stability and mounting discontent with the exploitative nature of the agreement, I resolved that it was time to walk away and pursue alternative avenues that would afford me greater autonomy and fairness in my career pursuits

Amidst the escalating tension, the situation reached a boiling point, culminating in a heated exchange between myself and the agent. In a surprising turn of events, the agent resorted to summoning the police, leading to the abrupt arrival of approximately six police cruisers at the scene. Suddenly, I found myself thrust into a moment of profound embarrassment as my rights seemed to be disregarded, and the specter of deportation loomed ominously overhead.

Seeking clarity in the midst of chaos, I confronted the police officers, demanding an explanation for the instructions the authorities to escort me out of the house along with all my belongings, destined for the airport. Refusing to succumb to coercion, I stood my ground, adamantly asserting my right to remain until the contractual agreement binding me to the agent was nullified.

Emphasizing the principle of mutual consent and contractual freedom, I insisted that just as I could not enter into the United States without a formal agreement or contract, I would not vacate the premises without the voluntary termination of the existing agreement. Determined to reclaim my autonomy and pursue alternative representation, I stood firm in my resolve to negotiate a resolution that would afford me the freedom to seek out a new agent independently.

Thirty minutes later, clutching the freshly minted clearance letter from the agent, I found myself en route to the airport, my departure imminent. Rushing through the bustling terminals, my agent's couple facilitated my swift check-in, liaising with the boarding supervisor to secure my seat on the next flight bound for Nairobi, Kenya, scheduled to depart within the hour. Laden with mixed emotions, I proceeded through the gates, bracing myself for the journey ahead. Yet, as fate would have it, a twist awaited me.

Moments later, a representative from the airline approached me with an unexpected proposition: the flight had been overbooked, and I was offered the chance to voluntarily defer my travel to the following day, with the promise of complimentary accommodations for the interim. Taken aback by the sudden turn of events, I sought counsel from my friend John Mwai, whose sage advice urged me to seize the opportunity. With his assurance that he and his friend Lee would retrieve me from the airport, I made the decision to accept the offer, setting in motion an unforeseen delay in my journey.

Within twenty minutes, I found myself back at the airport entrance, accompanied by Lee, my belongings in tow, as my flight plans were rearranged for a later date. Embracing the unexpected extension, I embarked on an additional two weeks of training under Lee's guidance. The subsequent weekend saw me competing once more, this time in a race separate from my agent's circuit, where I achieved a commendable second-place finish.

However, my success only seemed to intensify the ire of my agent, who questioned my sudden reappearance and the circumstances surrounding my participation in the race. Accusing me of unauthorized competition, my agent vowed to intervene, threatening to withhold my winnings. Fortunately, the clarity provided by the clearance letter I presented to the race organizers during the award ceremony swiftly resolved any doubts, ensuring my rightful participation and securing the payment of my winnings.

***

Excitement of reuniting with my running companions in Embu after my stint in the United States was palpable; everyone from

Embu wanting to learn from my experience in the Unites States. Other wanted to hear the good stories about how the world on the other side appears and what is the difference between the two worlds. Others sought connections to Athletes representatives however I could not deliver the bad experience abroad since with the bad experiences it ten times better than Embu. With renewed vigor, I resumed my training regimen, rejoining the Kenya Police training team as I used their good will gesture to prepare for the upcoming Beijing Marathon. Additionally, to my delight, I received the news of my selection for the World Championships, a testament to the dedication and effort I had poured into my athletic pursuits.

As the days passed, I remained steadfast in my commitment to excellence, knowing that the upcoming competitions demanded nothing short of my best. Each training session was approached with a sense of purpose and determination, as I honed my skills and endurance under the watchful guidance of my coaches and teammates.

The prospect of competing on the global stage filled me with a mix of anticipation and nervous energy. It was a culmination of years of hard work and sacrifice, an opportunity to showcase my talents and represent my country with pride. With each passing day, my focus sharpened, and my resolve hardened, knowing that I was inching closer to realizing my dreams of success on the international stage.

As I immersed myself in the rigorous training routines and preparations, I remained mindful of the significance of the events that lay ahead. Every mile logged, every sprint completed, brought me one step closer to my goals. With unwavering determination and unwavering support from my coaches and teammates, I embarked on the final leg of my journey towards the Beijing Marathon and the World Championships, ready to give it my all and leave everything on the track.

By this point in my career, I had meticulously crafted my own training methodology, tailored specifically to my needs and capabilities. Through years of experience and trial and error, I had come to understand that my body responded best to a structured approach divided into three distinct stages: the base pre-race training, the mid-training phase, and the intensive sessions.

In the base pre-race training phase, the focus was on laying a solid foundation for performance. Long runs and hill workouts were staples of this period, designed to build endurance and strength without introducing excessive intensity. Any attempts to push the pace prematurely were met with resistance, as the emphasis remained on gradually increasing mileage loads to prepare the body for the challenges ahead.

Transitioning into the mid-training phase, the intensity ramped up slightly as the focus shifted to incorporating speed work into the regimen. Long runs were complemented by fartlek speed plays, providing a blend of sustained effort and interval training. This phase served as a testing ground for the body, exposing it to gradual and randomized increments in speed to simulate race conditions and identify areas for improvement.

The final stage, the intensive sessions, represented the pinnacle of training intensity. Characterized by aggressive workouts that pushed the limits of physical and mental endurance, this phase demanded unwavering commitment and focus. Each session was designed to challenge both body and mind, pushing past comfort zones to unlock peak performance potential.

Through careful planning and dedication to each phase of training, I sought to optimize my preparation for competition, knowing that success on the track hinged upon meticulous attention to detail and unwavering determination.

In that eventful year, I returned to the Beijing Marathon in October with renewed determination. As the race kicked off, a group of Chinese runners surged ahead with remarkable speed right from the start. Initially, along with other elite runners assumed that they would fade away before reaching the halfway mark, especially considering that the race included both marathon and half marathon runners starting together.

To my surprise, I had been under the impression that I was leading the pack since from our point of view we saw no one ahead of us; also we never realized that the lead vehicle was not with us all through the course of the race. It soon became apparent that the winner and the second-place runner had surged ahead, finishing a remarkable six minutes ahead of us; as I crossed the finish line, I found myself being handed the third position award after finishing the race in two hours and thirteen minutes. It was a moment of both pride and astonishment.

Despite narrowly missing out on the top spots, the experience served as a valuable lesson in the unpredictable nature of competitive racing. It highlighted the importance of pacing oneself effectively and remaining vigilant throughout the entirety of the race, ensuring that no opportunities for advancement were missed. With this newfound insight, I returned to the drawing board, eager to refine my strategies and continue striving for excellence in future competitions.

Upon my return to Kenya, I opted not to participate in any marathons the following year. However, John Mwai approached me with a proposal to train together in Nyahururu, where an agent from Canada had shown interest in representing me. Intrigued by the opportunity, I agreed to join John and we set up camp at his home in Nyahururu.

For four weeks, we dedicated ourselves to intense training sessions. However, my health took a sudden turn for the worse, and I found myself falling ill and losing a significant amount of weight. Concerned for my well-being, I confided in John, expressing my need to return to Embu due to my deteriorating health.

Back in Embu, my body appeared depleted of essential nutrients, and I began to experience extreme weakness and fatigue. Even the simplest tasks became challenging, and I struggled to get out of bed.

As days passed, my condition worsened. My complexion grew pale, and my skin became rough to the touch. Faced with the harsh reality of my declining health, I knew that I was teetering on the brink of collapse and potentially facing a life-threatening situation. In that moment, I couldn't help but contemplate the possibility of bidding farewell to my loved ones, realizing that each passing moment brought me closer to the edge of survival.

I generously distributed all my running gears to those around me, including my brother, giving away anything I considered valuable to anyone who could make use of it. Gradually, I found myself possessing only the bare essentials needed to sustain my life for the days ahead. Despite not being on medication or experiencing any significant pain, I felt immensely weak and fragile.

I sought medical attention from a clinician who conducted tests to get what my hemoglobin levels would reveal. It turned out that I was severely malnourished. It was merely three months after my exit from USA and I was deeply stressed and lost vital clues and instincts. I could not differentiate hunger and thirst; I never felt hungry of in need to eat. I couldn't eat a full meal to completion and that was my main cause of weakness.

The doctor told me that I have no illness and all that the blood work revealed was lack of proper nourishment. He asked me what kind of food I eat, how and who prepares it. He instructed me to eat two meals a day and to not resume running for another one month.

With that reality the next day I woke up with a newfound determination. I instructed my brother to purchase goat bones for soup, hoping to harness whatever nourishment they could provide. The bones were boiled continuously for approximately two hours, extracting every bit of goodness they held. I consumed the soup slowly, sipping it repeatedly as though it were my lifeline. Over the course of the next three days, it became my sole source of sustenance, providing me with whatever nourishment I could manage to intake.

Remarkably, after just four days of this regimen, I began to experience a remarkable improvement in my condition. I regained the strength to rise from my bed, and my appetite gradually returned, allowing me to consume regular food once again. With each passing day, my energy levels increased, and within two weeks, I felt capable enough to resume light training, signaling a significant turnaround in my health and well-being.

***

After three months of recovery and basic training, I received a call from John, who excitedly informed me that Lee, along with a friend, was planning to visit Kenya to collaborate on establishing a running camp. Thrilled to be part of such a significant venture, I eagerly embraced the opportunity. We convened with John in Nairobi to lay the groundwork for the project, which included visiting the Kenya Athletics Association office (KAAA) to introduce our innovative idea to the sports administration. Together, we meticulously planned the logistics of the camp, from selecting the ideal location to devising strategies for athlete recruitment.

During our preparations, John and I divided responsibilities according to our strengths and expertise. John took charge of the camp's general administration, overseeing its day-to-day operations, ensuring sustainability, and managing accommodations. Meanwhile, I assumed responsibility for all financial matters, including budgeting for the club and handling official paperwork local and international and recruitments of athletes. We collaborated closely on development of training programs to ensure a well-rounded approach to nurturing talent.

After careful consideration, we decided to establish the camp in Jambini village, nestled within the picturesque surroundings of Ambadare. With our roles clearly defined and our plans in motion, we embarked on this venture with enthusiasm and determination, eager to create a nurturing environment where athletes could thrive and reach their full potential.

Inevitably, the typical human urge to vie for personal interests reared its head within our sports camp, resulting in a profound rift between John and me. This divide was fueled by his military colleagues, whose ulterior motive was to assert control over the training camp in a military fashion. The discord began to surface during our athlete recruitment efforts. Initially, John and I had agreed to recruit a diverse mix of athletes from various backgrounds - including the army, police, local community, and independent runners - to ensure a balanced demographic.

However, it soon became apparent that John had tipped off numerous military acquaintances about our recruitment exercise and the hotels where we would be lodging on different days. To my surprise, individuals from the American contingent, seemingly unaware of our carefully planned strategy, eagerly engaged with anyone who presented themselves as runners. I distinctly remember an incident in Nyahururu where John orchestrated a scenario with his friends. He arranged to meet me for a private discussion at a coffee shop near our hotel, while his friend feigned coincidence by appearing to search for both of us. Seizing the opportunity, they introduced themselves to the interested Americans.

By the end of the meeting, a list of army runners had been offered contracts and were poised to join the residential training camp at Njambini. This orchestrated maneuvering left me feeling disillusioned and marginalized within the camp, as my efforts to foster inclusivity and diversity were overshadowed by covert agendas.

Following the recruitment of runners for the Njambini training camp, we devised tailored training strategies to suit each athlete's needs, ranging from track events to marathons. Morning runs were conducted collectively, while daytime programs varied according to the specific requirements of individual runners. In preparation for the London Marathon scheduled for April of that year, I meticulously planned my training regimen. I diligently increased mileage and incorporated speed work, benefiting from the assistance of the newly recruited young men.

Upon my arrival at the hotel, a package containing sports apparel with my name on it was delivered to my room; two days after arrival my then manager arrived and come to my room for a brief meeting. As is customary, anything bearing one's name and related to their profession is typically assumed to be theirs. I had unpacked and organize the items to fit into my smaller bag. However, when my manager arrived at the hotel room, he expressed disappointment that I had unpacked the packages without waiting for him. Nevertheless, he inspected the items and took away some of the things he deemed necessary.

Unfortunately, my performance in the race did not meet expectations. I managed to stay with the leading pack until the 25-kilometer mark, where disaster struck. Unaware of a speed bump ahead, I inadvertently stepped on it with greater force than anticipated. In an attempt to adjust my stride, I overcompensated and arched backward, resulting in excruciating pain shooting up my spine and immobilizing my left leg from the hip down. I struggled to continue running, eventually resorting to walking for three kilometers before resuming a running pace. Despite the setback, I completed the marathon in 2 hours and 39 minutes.

The day after the marathon, I boarded a British Airways flight home bound, and John awaited me at the airport. I caught up with John at the airport who was curious about my experience in London before heading to Embu. Before parting ways john asked me if I was given any apparel to bring to the team of which I replied no.

Five days later, upon my return to Njambini, I was met with an unexpected situation. John had lied to the entire team that I have their training gears, including shoes and tracksuits for everyone, and would bring them upon my return to the camp from Embu. This revelation left me feeling a mix of amusement and frustration, as I realized something dubious was unfolding. After three days of contemplation, I decided to pack my belongings and leave this mediocre class of mentality and go home to Embu.

As I made preparations to leave, several runners approached me, pleading with me not to abandon them in the midst of what they described as a chaotic environment led by leaders lacking in moral and ethical sportsmanship.

Feeling a profound sense of responsibility for the success of the young athletes under my care, I made the decision to humble myself and return to the camp, extending my stay to continue assisting wherever necessary. However, a month later, circumstances took a dire turn as the camp faced a shortage of food and funds ran dry. John informed me that the manager in the USA claimed to have sent money to my bank account urgently needed for food supplies.

Acting swiftly, I traveled to Naivasha town to access the funds, only to discover there was no money in my account. Upon contacting the agent in the USA, I was shocked to learn that the funds had been sent to John's account, The agent said he has a letter of resolution from both John and me and he is implementing whatever the resolute was to fill the void after my relinquishment of financial responsibility; he added that a document bearing my purported signature was in his possession from our weekly administrative meeting. The agent questioned my inquiry, insinuating that I had willingly abdicated my duties at the camp.

Upon my return to Jambini, I confronted John regarding the discrepancy, but he denied any knowledge of such a letter, labeling the agent's claims as untrue. Frustrated and disillusioned by the situation, I made the decision to leave the camp behind, returning to Embu the following day. I composed an email to the manager, expressing my intention to remain under his management but to pursue individual training at home.

***

Several months later, I received an invitation to the USA for a series of road races, an opportunity I eagerly embraced. I competed in several road races in the Unites States until I felt a need to return back to Kenya. However, before my return to Kenya, I was entrusted with the task of accompanying two female athletes from Jambini to Florida for their inaugural international races. My task was to travel with them from Philadelphia to Florida. Arriving in Philadelphia on a Thursday evening from Nairobi Kenya, we swiftly departed for Florida the following night. Their appearance at the St. Petersburg 10-miler was marked by palpable fatigue and astonishment, given the novelty of their international debut. While I managed to secure a sixth-place finish, both athletes were forced to withdraw from the race due to exhaustion and the abrupt change in climate.

Following the race, on Sunday night, we made our way back to Pennsylvania, where we were met by the manager, who had undisclosed plans in store. After picking us up from the airport, he concentrated on the young girls for a while asking them what had happened and why they dropped out of the race. Sooner the agent launched into a relentless tirade toward myself; bombarding me with insults and obscure parables, leaving me bewildered and unsure of the purpose behind his lecture. Upon arriving at the house, he convened a clandestine meeting with some of the runners while I retired to my room, seeking respite.

The following day coincided with the birthday of one of the runners, an occasion slated for celebration. We undertook the task of adorning the venue with vibrant flowers and preparing traditional Kenyan dishes, showcasing our culinary skills.

The aftermath of the party left a palpable tension lingering in the air, with everyone seemingly on edge, striving to conform to the managers' expectations. The subsequent day saw an early departure of the athletes, leaving me alone to grapple with my thoughts. Sensing the need for solitude and self-care, I made the decision to forego my weekend race and prioritize my well-being.

Meanwhile, the athletes embarked on a journey to New Jersey for a race where they encountered an intriguing individual named JL

Seymore. The exchange of contacts culminated in Seymore being extended an invitation to visit our residence in Pennsylvania. Eager to connect further, Seymore wasted no time and promptly arrived at the house on the agreed-upon day, finding himself in the company of the athletes who had initially invited him.

That day I slept late and woke up around nine in the morning. After breakfast I returned and chilled in my room. At around eleven in the morning one of the athletes come to my room and told me there is a visitor and they don't know what to tell him. I walked to the living room and there comes a smiling face of JL Seymore. Seymore was well-spoken individual who exhibited a profound familiarity with me, having observed my performances in races. While we exchanged few words suddenly all other runner slipped through the backdoor and disappeared. JL Seymore and myself were not aware about the behaviors of the runners who had extended his invitation to our quarters. I found myself at a loss, unaware of their plans. Advising Seymore to await their return if they had scheduled a meeting, I observed the unfolding events with a sense of curiosity and apprehension.

In Seymore's company, I endeavored to extend every hospitality, offering him meals, tea, and a taste of Kenyan dishes. However, our interaction took an unexpected turn when the assistant manager, a female, made an unusual appearance at the house. Inquiring about a specific runner, she sought to speak with them, to which I could only respond truthfully that I was unaware of their whereabouts. Determined not to leave Seymore alone or abruptly dismiss him, I remained in his company until he realized his impending departure and bid us farewell, leaving his contact details for further communication.

It wasn't until later that evening all the other athletes arrived and with no words, to me each retired to their respective bed. The full extent of the situation didn't become apparent until two days later which were unveiled during a group meeting. Unbeknownst to me, the runners had deceitfully fabricated a story, falsely alleging that I had invited another agent to recruit them, an act deemed unlawful under the IAAF's anti-poaching guidelines. This concocted narrative was the reason the assistant manager's visit to our residence on that material day seeking confirmation of these claims.

In this unexpected and clandestine meeting, I found myself confronted with the most ludicrous accusations I had ever faced in my athletic career. The manager began by alleging I had plans to trade athletes to a black agent whom I invited to the house. This was purely false as I failed the way to counter their already perceived guilt, my mind was preoccupied with the childish in the entire clubs system and their level of maturity. The second claim was that the female athletes who accompanied me to Florida had reported that I took them to a disco club the night before the race, insinuating that this contributed to their poor performance. However, this accusation was utterly baseless. It turned out that John was remotely coordinating and planning my expulsion from the club while he was miles away in Africa. Years later the same athletes confessed that they were coerced to lie and this was done the one day after our return from Florida. They claimed that the fear of being sent back to Kenya outweighed the simple notion of lying.

The next allegation leveled against me was equally absurd – that every day I failed to greet the junior athletes with morning salutations. This accusation seemed trivial and lacked any logical basis, leading me to dismiss it as childish and unworthy of serious consideration.

Lastly, I was confronted with complaints from two men I had recruited from my hometown, Nthua and Nyenje. Nthua claimed to dislike me because he perceived me as unsmiling, I don't volunteer greetings in the morning and he deemed me as selfish, while Nyenje expressed discomfort in my presence and advocated for my removal from the organization if he were to remain part of it. These accusations felt unjust and unfounded, leaving me bewildered by the sudden turn of events and the apparent hostility directed towards mc.

Looking back, I realized the significant role I played in Nthua's journey to success. I remember funding his passport and putting in the effort to secure his spot in the running club, knowing the challenges he faced in finding representation. It was disheartening to see him thriving in the USA without acknowledging the support I had provided. However, I chose not to take it personally and found peace within myself.

On the other hand, Nyenje, who had excelled in shorter distances and remained undefeated in all his races, had approached me for assistance over a year prior. Despite his coach's efforts in Embu and various attempts to secure opportunities, he remained overlooked. I had assured the agent that he is a good runner and worth investing on. Here we stand at this moment turning against me, metaphorically stretching my arms on the cross of condemnation and marking where to place the crucifixion nail.

In moments of trial, I turned to my faith, seeking wisdom and guidance to navigate these challenges.

In the face of allegations and pressure to defend myself, I chose to stand firm in my convictions. I refused to engage in petty arguments or prove anyone right or wrong. Instead, I asserted my confidence in who I am and what I stood for. This was not just about clearing my name; it was about preserving my integrity and refusing to compromise my principles. With Johns previous acts in Njambini, I was aware that he was the one operating this machine remotely together with his military team mates! I was aware on my values and my potential and this was just a waste of time fighting to remain in this man eaters management.

I knew that my running experience and knowledge of athletics far surpassed those around me. I was aware that my experience was what brough me to this club; I came here to share my expertise. Any attempt to discredit or undermine me was a grave mistake to my career. With clarity of mind, I demanded a clearance letter devoid of baseless accusations so I could leave without further tarnishing my reputation.

Despite the pressure from both athletes and management to accept fault and move on, I remained steadfast in my stance. Two days later, I found myself at the airport, escorted by my manager. As soon as he handed my passport, I opened it. The first thing I noticed was the visa being written over with a black Marker pen the word "Cancelled". Upon asking him why he damaged my passport and if this was appropriate thing he could do. He said he did that to protect his company and to make sure I will never step again to the United States of America. I didn't say anything, I boarded the flight thinking about it all the way until I arrived home. I didn't know what I had done wrong however I was aware of one thing. My reticence and introvert nature is mostly mistaken and people get poor impression of my personality. A fact I realized I have to live with this bias all my life.

***

Returning to Embu, I found myself grappling with a mix of emotions: anger, hurt, and a sense of betrayal. It was disheartening to feel singled out after all the effort I had put into building one of the strongest running teams in the country. Despite the setback, I refused to let negativity consume me.

Having faced setbacks from two agents in the past two years, it was crucial for me to showcase my true worth. Despite their attempts to undermine my prospects, I remained steadfast in my determination to demonstrate my abilities on the global stage. However, despite my efforts, my participation in the Beijing Marathon that year faced unexpected obstacles. Surprisingly, I did not receive the official invitation from China, raising concerns about what went on to Beijing Marathon race organizer; I didn't know what influence my previous agents had toward Beijing that caused them to overlook my participation that year.

I didn't give up on any of my dreams, as long as I knew how to train and as long as there was no injuries hindering my progress; I felt there was room for thriving.

Several weeks later, JL Seymore reached out to me with an unexpected opportunity. He had initiated a petition to represent runners, and he wanted me to be a part of it. JL Seymore knew that I was expelled from the previous management for my hospitality during his visit. He was aware I was humiliated for being a true man against the odds. Additionally, he sought my guidance in establishing a running club akin to the one I had previously created. Embracing this chance to make a positive impact, I eagerly accepted his offer and began scouting for athletes who would be a good fit for the new club.

The prospect of starting afresh was invigorating, especially knowing that the new club would train in the same location as the Kenyan Cross Country team, right in my hometown. With renewed determination, I set out to lay the foundation for a community of runners dedicated to excellence and mutual support.

Mr. Seymore entrusted me with the necessary funds to establish the running club, including registration as an athlete's representative agent with the KAAA. With these resources at hand,

I embarked on recruiting talented runners from various events across the country. Within a span of two months, our official training camp commenced at St. Marks Teachers College.

World Championship management established its base at St. Mark Teachers College in Embu, Kenya. Managing a total of seventeen runners, I ensured that they reported diligently every day, providing weekly reports to Mr. Seymore as he pursued international races for them. Meanwhile, amidst these managerial responsibilities, I remained focused on my personal goal of training for the Beijing Marathon for the sixth time. This endeavor posed a significant challenge as it was imperative for me to prove my capability to perform at the international level. I invited Silvan to join us as our coach with a decent pay. Soon after realizing how much money was involved in running the camp, his attitude changed, and some dark ideas began to creep in.

JL Seymore hinted to me about the letter that had been secretly handed to him by Silvan during his visit to Kenya.

He started writing false claims to JL Seymore, alleging that he (Silvan) did not believe that I was paying athletes their dues every month. Firstly, there was no athlete entitled to any payment from us, and secondly, these claims were poisoning both the manager and the athletes. Following these unfounded claims from Silvan, it was time to let him go and replace him with Dan Muchoki.

****

David Okeyo, the KAAA general secretary, summoned me to Nairobi to discuss matters concerning the ongoing conflict between myself and the previous agent. In his office, he revealed that KAAA had initiated an investigation into the agent's conduct. Additionally, he presented me with unexpected news: a special invitation had been extended by the international community for the Pyongyang Marathon. This invitation marked the inaugural occurrence of such an event, requiring the participation of four runners, consisting of two men and two women. To my surprise, I was entrusted with leading the delegation of marathon runners. Instead of the designated composition of two men and two women, three men and only one woman were sent to represent our country.

Upon arrival at the marathon, it became apparent that the delegation did not align with the initial instructions. This discrepancy added a layer of complexity to our participation in the event.

The journey to Pyongyang began with a stopover in Beijing, where we spent three days before continuing to the capital of North Korea. Upon arrival at the airport, we walked from the aircraft to the terminal, clutching our passports. We were asked to present all documents and wait for four hours while officials meticulously inspected our bags, translating any foreign writings into Korean. Exhausted, we found ourselves sprawled on the terminal floor by the time the inspection concluded.

Our experience in Pyongyang was equally surreal. Assigned a female guide proficient in basic English, we quickly realized her role was to monitor us around the clock. From the airport, we embarked on a drive to the hotel, the distance of which remains a blur in my memory because the heat inside the shuttle bus forced me to a nice momentous slumber. The airport itself seemed isolated, surrounded by vast expanses of rice fields, stretching endlessly into the horizon.

Throughout our stay, the guide's presence was constant, though she would discreetly be replaced by another obscure agent after our bedtime to monitor the hotel and the flat landscape surrounding. On our first morning run, we often found ourselves uncertain of which direction to take, our guide's absence leaving us feeling disoriented.

Despite the challenges and surveillance, we found a small sense of freedom in the evening hours when our daytime guide bid us goodnight, only for her replacement to quietly take over. It was during these moments, gazing out of our hotel window at nine o'clock each night, that we caught glimpses of our guides swapping shifts.

By the third day, a Monday, we finally settled into a comfortable routine for our runs. After five days of adjusting to our surroundings, our ninety-minute run felt like a significant breakthrough. While our presence in Pyongyang was ostensibly about engaging with the international community, for me, running remained the focal point of my existence, requiring a deep understanding of every aspect.

Eager to learn more about the upcoming event, we requested a meeting with the Elite Athlete Coordinator on Monday. However, we were informed that the coordinator would only be available for a briefing on Thursday. In the meantime, we were encouraged to explore recreational venues and amusement parks.

Tuesday was dedicated to touring the city's historical sites, including the birthplace of the late Kim Jong-il, a monumental statue in his honor at the visitors' park, and a captivating performance at the theater. The highlight of the day was undoubtedly the panoramic view from the five-hundred-meter sky-drive tower, offering breathtaking vistas of Pyongyang and its surroundings.

Before arriving in North Korea, my perception of the country was shaped by sensationalized news reports portraying it as a desolate jungle, where residents struggled with hunger and deprivation. The images I had seen in newspapers depicted depopulated towns devoid of paved roads, telephone lines, or even basic amenities like televisions. These narratives painted a bleak picture, with stories of people resorting to eating grass due to severe food shortages. Naturally, I was intrigued to witness the purported "dark side" of North Korea for myself.

However, upon arrival, we were confronted with a starkly different reality. Contrary to expectations, we found ourselves in a modernized country with all the amenities commonly found in the Western world. The streets were lined with bustling activity, and infrastructure resembled that of any developed nation

Despite this, our experience in North Korea was not devoid of cultural differences and peculiarities that reminded us of the unique nature of this society.

Our experience in North Korea was marked by a series of eye-opening revelations that challenged our accustomed way of life. The first distinction that was visible was the presence of hand waving traffic police. The second visible distinction was their shops had very selected items that fell short of foreign good. It was a surprising revelation that challenged my preconceived notions about the country. One outstanding North Koreans state agency behavior was the meticulously monitored nature of our activities, with a visible guide during the day and an obscure sentry overseeing us at night. This constant surveillance was a reminder of the tight control exerted by the authorities over the populace.

The communal responsibility in North Korea was truly remarkable. Each morning, the roads were meticulously swept by hand, with every adult assigned their own spot to clean by 6 a.m. This dedication to cleanliness and order was evident in the bustling activities that commenced early in the morning, with individuals carrying out various tasks and responsibilities, contributing to the overall upkeep of their community.

One more of the highlights of my time in North Korea was undoubtedly the seafood cuisine. Every meal consisted entirely of seafood, and I was amazed by the variety available. We enjoyed a wide range of fish from the ocean, to the extent that I couldn't remember having the same fish meal twice in three days. The abundance and diversity of seafood meant that by the time I encountered the same fish again in my meal, I had already forgotten its taste from the previous dish.

Another startling discovery was the extreme rationing of basic necessities, particularly water. Water availability was limited to specific times of the day, with narrow windows between six to eight in the morning, noon to one in the afternoon, and seven to nine in the evening. This stringent rationing system underscored the scarcity mindset prevalent in the country.

Television viewing was similarly regulated, with programming heavily skewed towards glorifying the country's ruler and promoting anti-American sentiments. Each viewer was allocated an extra hour of viewing time, albeit within the confines of state-approved content.

Communications posed yet another challenge, as the telephone system operated on an outdated method requiring users to request the desired number and await their turn. This antiquated system made it cumbersome to establish contact with individuals outside of North Korea, such as my manager in the US and David Okeyo in Kenya. Despite our initial efforts, navigating these communication barriers proved to be a formidable task.

On Wednesday night, the event coordinator brought race information to our attention, including details about the race route, bib numbers, and water bottles. She also emphasized what she called a special moment for international runners, highlighting the array of awards available, which piqued our interest.

Among these prizes were a silver cup, glamorous flowers, delightful chocolate bars, and the chance to meet with a delegate of the king. However, I was more concerned about the appearance money that had been promised from Nairobi when we accepted the deal.

We also pressed on for details about the prize money for the events. Despite my inquiries, the coordinator repeatedly emphasized that money was not important; rather, participation was paramount for the North Korean people to showcase admiration to their leader. According to her all that she cared for was pleasing their king. I started regretting my prior commitment to run Paris marathon that weekend of which I was urged to switch to this opportunity and represent Kenya in North Korea with a promise of three thousand dollar as appearance money and undisclosed prize money. The coordinator left without divulging the amount of the winning prize, but it became evident that there were no appearance fees included in the arrangement.

I requested to make a call to Kenya and to JL Seymore, my American agent. However, I was informed that I can only be allowed as long as

I submit the names of the persons I want to call, their phone numbers, my relationship to them, and what I want to talk about—all in writing. When I got JL on the phone, the audio was faint, and it was obvious that it was wiretapped. The guide lady was next to me, listening to everything I said, and it was strictly limited to three minutes. I informed JL that we had little information about the winning prize money or awards. JL was displeased with my tale of events, but time was limited. From that moment, I decided not to run to save my energy, perhaps for a good marathon the following month.

***

The remaining three days were designated for attending various events hosted specifically for international delegates by Pyongyang. I grew weary of the constant touring, and from that day on, I opted out of the tours that the other team members participated in. Instead, I chose to stay in the hotel most of the time. On Thursday, we were informed that we were invited for a briefing message in the evening.

During the briefing, I directed my inquiry about the prize structure to the individual who seemed to be in charge of race affairs. He pointed me to a female employee who accessed the file and informed me that the winning prize was one thousand five hundred US dollars. Her response seemed uncertain, as if she struggled to interpret the figures or it was a mistake since such prizes were unheard of in Korean running history. It appeared to her that such money could not be handled by an individual and not in North Korea. Despite my repeated questions, she reassured me that it was indeed the correct amount.

We resorted back to our hotel and continued with our daily food endeavors.

During our stay, we were treated to a wide array of soups, ranging from seafood soup to beef soup, as well as plant-based and even artificial soups. Each soup offered a unique flavor profile, blending authentic local tastes with innovative culinary creations.

Additionally, we were introduced to a variety of breads made from different seeds, a departure from the common wheat grain breads we were accustomed to. To accompany our meals, we were served Chinese tea, both black and green varieties, adding to the diverse culinary experience.

On race day, which fell on a Sunday, my disillusionment with North Korea had reached its peak. The restrictions on our movement, confined only to permitted areas, and the pervasive idolization of King Jong Un on television made the experience dull and suffocating. The deadened atmosphere, with inactive televisions, phones, and water supply for most of the day, only added to the sense of monotony. With my decision firmly made, I resolved not to participate in what I saw as a sham race. While my teammates went through their usual pre-race rituals on Thursday, Friday, and Saturday, I abstained from training, deeming it pointless to exert myself for a mere one thousand five hundred dollars.

As race day dawned I remained resolute. The weather was favorable, with temperatures around 16 degrees Celsius and minimal winds. The flat course, interspersed with gentle slopes, promised an enjoyable race, but my indifference persisted. Citing the desperation from my team mates who pleaded with me to join and perhaps drop out after several kilometers, I opted to use the event as a training session. With this last minute decision I decided to act unusual as possible so that I don't feel as my energy is wasted, with the intention to withdraw soon after.

By the 10-kilometer mark, we had covered the distance in 30 minutes.

Realizing that none of my teammates were trailing behind me, I intentionally slowed down to allow them to catch up. After a brief period, they joined me, but it was evident that they lacked the stamina to maintain the pace. Concerned about their well-being, I encouraged them to push forward, but one teammate confessed to having no energy left to accelerate.

Inquiring about the others, I learned that one had dropped out at the 5-kilometer mark, while the whereabouts of the female athlete remained unknown.

Reflecting on the wasteful expenditure incurred on our tour of North Korea, I felt a sense of frustration. Despite the resources invested, none of us seemed poised to finish in the top ten. Determined to salvage some pride for our Kenyan team, I decided to push on towards the finish line. Breaking away from the pack, I surged ahead, leaving my teammate behind. With none from the group in pursuit, I soon caught up with the lead group comprised of two North Koreans, two South Koreans and one Chinese runner.

As we pressed on together, no one dropped out until we reached the 25-kilometer mark, at which point the Chinese runner began to fall behind. By the time we hit the 30-kilometer mark, the two South Koreans initiated speed intervals in an attempt to break away from me. Despite their efforts, we all maintained the increased pace, and by the time we reached 33 kilometers, they too started to lag behind.

Left with only two Northern Korean runners, we were accompanied by a convoy of four motorbikes. These bikes provided support, with one positioned in front, one on each side, and one carrying drinks for the Korean runner trailing behind us. The coach, situated on the left motorbike, continuously communicated with the athletes in Korean.

At the 36-kilometer mark, one of the Korean runners couldn't sustain the pace and fell back, leaving just two of us in the lead. Despite conserving energy throughout the race, I couldn't shake off the fear of being overtaken from behind.

Sensing an opportunity at the 39-kilometer mark, I strategically positioned myself just one step behind the Korean runner. As his motorbike aid attempted to pass him a special drink, he fumbled to grab the bottle several times. Recognizing the challenge, I swiftly took the bottle from the aid, ensuring he got the energy he needed but not to beat me; I drunk a few gulps of the drink before passing it to the runner with assumption that they can't feed him poison while he is running. whatever they are giving him must have been something well thought of.

With only two kilometers to go, I felt as though I had just begun the race, and within moments, I spotted the 41-kilometer marker. With renewed vigor, I launched into a massive sprint, fueled by the remaining reserves of energy. Crossing the finish line, I achieved a course record of two hours, eleven minutes, and 5 seconds.

After crossing the finish line, an unusual sensation enveloped me; I didn't feel as though I had just completed a marathon. Reflecting on my performance, three factors stood out: rest, seafood, and an unexpected drink. In the days leading up to the race, I prioritized rest and avoided extensive social activities that might have taxed my energy reserves, particularly given my introverted nature.

Another potential factor was the abundance of seafood in the Korean diet, rich in vitamins and natural iron elements crucial for body functioning. The variety of underwater delicacies I consumed likely provided a nutritional boost that contributed to my performance.

However, the most intriguing element was the mysterious drink I ingested during the race. While it wasn't intended for me, I seized the opportunity to aid a fellow runner who struggled to retrieve it from the support motorcycle. The concoction had a subtle salty taste, hinting at the presence of electrolytes, and a potent herbal flavor, possibly derived from ginseng. Its potency was such that it significantly reduced my sweating, leaving me almost dry by the race's end.

One of my male teammates managed to secure the 34th position, a commendable feat given the competition. Unfortunately, the second male runner dropped out during the race, as did the female athlete. Despite our mixed results, the award ceremony proceeded promptly after the race, and we swiftly returned to our hotel to prepare for departure from North Korea.

Exiting the country proved to be another challenge, as there were only two flights per week from China to North Korea; on Mondays and Thursdays. Since it was already after the race on Sunday and booking required a minimum of three days in advance, Monday departures were out of the question; we stayed three more days before out flight to Beijing, another one day in China before boarding Ethiopian Airline to Adis Ababa and a final leg to Nairobi.

***

Back in Embu, training resumed at Kigari Embu with all the athletes under my care pulling up their socks to match their master. The entire camp became a beehive of activity, with runners motivated by my performance in North Korea. At that moment, I was managing seventeen athletes, and they were all eager to elevate their training to match my standards.

Before long, David Okeyo sent Dan Muchoki with news about an invitation to the Beijing Marathon. They had taken note of my performance in North Korea and were confident that I was in top form. This marked the beginning of one of the most grueling training periods I had ever experienced. With the Kenyan team's arrival at St. Marks Teachers College, I had the privilege of training alongside legends such as Paul Tergat, Eliud Kipchoge, Patrick Ivuti, Sammy Korir, and others.

During this time, my American agent traveled to Kenya to witness our training firsthand. He arrived one week before the National Championship, allowing him to observe the entire national team selection process. It was during this period that Dan Muchoki served as our camp coach, overseeing our preparations for the upcoming challenges.

One eventful day, JL Seymore decided to join us on a long run.

The running started from St. Mark College to the edge of Mt. Kenya Forest and back, a total eighteen-kilometer route; as usual we gathered at the gate, counted heads, and set off. JL Seymore kept with us for the first 4 kilometers before falling behind.

When we reached the 9-kilometer mark and began our descent back, we encountered JL Seymore, who insisted on continuing to the edge of the forest like everyone else. After completing the run, showering, and having breakfast, I retired to my room, momentarily forgetting about my manager's absence at breakfast.

Suddenly, a runner burst into the room, informing me that there was a message for me at the main gate. Rushing to the main gate and upon answering the phone, it was JL Seymore on the line, calling from a stranger's phone to explain that he was lost and exhausted, approximately fifty minutes away on foot.

Without hesitation, I grabbed my car keys, called one of the closest athlete in our camp Wilson Kagiri to join me for this rescue mission; and we drove north to Kianjokoma market before heading south toward Ngurueri village on Kibogi road. We found JL sitting near a homestead, conversing with villagers who were amazed by his act of kindness.

JL recounted how he had followed the expected route to the edge of the forest, then turned around running back passing the camp until he arrived at main road to Embu - Meru road. At that moment he realizes he had passed the training camp by 5 kilometers. Turning back, he ran for 30 minutes; again, going past the camp for the second time arriving at Kianjokoma market for the third time.

At the main junction near Kianjokoma market, all he remembered was that the entrance to the camp was on the right side of the road, therefore turning right, he headed south toward Ngurueri, yet another way off the course, running for another 6 kilometers until he encountered a steep hill. It was then that he realized he was lost, having already run for three hours. By the hillside, he encountered a young boy pushing a bicycle laden with water containers. On seeing how the boy struggled pushing the bicycle up hill, JL regained energy to help this young African kid. He felt mercy for this African way of life. He decided to chip in and help the young boy. After helping the boy, JL asked for assistance, leading him to a family who assisted him with a cell phone to contact St. Mark's College for help with his precarious distressing situation.

After JL's departure, my training reached new heights as Beijing became our main focus. KAAA had decided to include one of my athletes, Onesmus Nzioka, with me on this trip to China. Onesmus proved to be an exceptional training partner, exceeding all expectations in our preparations. We tackled long runs on Mondays, covering a massive 2.50-minute route. Our speed workouts included grueling 20-kilometer track intervals in single sessions. Fartleks were executed on a specific route starting from the camp and ending just minutes away.

As the race approached, Onesmus began to feel the strain and requested a few days off before our journey to Beijing in October. Despite this, he arrived in Beijing in peak condition, showing remarkable fitness and even outperforming me during training sessions. However, during the race, he seemed to defer to me for guidance.

At the 40-kilometer mark, a Chinese runner had surged ahead, leading by 30 seconds and we couldn't both catch him; Onesimus finished second, while I crossed the line in third place.

***

Upon our return to Embu, the team celebrated our performance in Beijing. Meanwhile, JL organized for a team of four athletes to compete in various races across the USA, ranging from 5 kilometers to half marathons. He also extended the invitation for me to join them in the United States. Again, running road races was never my favorite trend so after several months I decided to return back to Embu awaiting my next marathon assignment.

Returning to Embu from the USA, I was surprised to find that several athletes were missing from the camp. Upon inquiring about their whereabouts, I was informed that they had gone to visit relatives over the weekend and would return soon. Little did I know that during the same weekend, there was a grand prix event taking place in Brussels.

Shortly thereafter, I received a call from JL Seymore, who asked about one of our steeplechase athlete. I explained that to my best knowledge he had family issues to attend to at home but would be returning to the camp shortly. It was only later that I learned JL Seymore had seen the results of the same athlete competing in Europe.

I was astonished and deeply ashamed. Here we were, providing support for these athletes in terms of food, shelter, and coaching, yet someone else had represented them without consideration for the commitment they had made to our camp. It was a stark reminder of the challenges we faced in safeguarding our athletes' interests in a competitive and sometimes ruthless environment.

However, unsettling rumors began circulating at Kigali. It was alleged that other agents were attempting to poach our athletes, with whispers suggesting that our coach had been bribed to facilitate their departure while we were away in the US. Despite lacking concrete evidence, both JL and I were deeply concerned about the situation.

Faced with these troubling developments, we made the difficult decision to close the camp entirely. It was a drastic measure, but we felt it was necessary to protect the integrity of our team and ensure the well-being of our athletes.

The decision to close the camp marked a new chapter of adversity for me. While an American agent had instructed the full closure of the residential camp, it was met with resistance from those who had benefited from its existence. Hostility ensued, with some runners refusing to leave the camp, others filing reports at the police station claiming they had been unfairly instructed to go home, and some even absconding with furniture that I had purchased for their living quarters.

While closing the camp, I had received an invitation to run in the Nagoya Marathon in Japan. In three days, I was in Japan and upon returning, I found myself approached by a few police officers while doing shopping in a small Manyatta market; the police offices knew me very well. They informed me that the Officer in Charge of the Station (OCS) was seeking to speak with me urgently. They emphasized the importance of complying with his request.

Feeling a sense of unease, I agreed to accompany them to the police station. Little did I know that this simple visit would lead to me being treated as a suspect and ultimately placed in police cell. It was a sudden and shocking turn of events that left me bewildered and uncertain about what lay ahead.

Suddenly, they grabbed me and handcuffed me.

I was completely unaware that there was a scheme underway to end my running career for doing my job with integrity.

Spending the next two days in a police cell was a bewildering and emotionally taxing experience. It soon became apparent that those who benefited with the camps existence harbored resentment since its closure and had orchestrated my predicament. Rumors circulated that individuals with influential connections within the police force were being leveraged to teach me a lesson.

Feeling unjustly targeted and deeply upset by the turn of events, I found myself overcome with emotions while confined in the cell. The realization that I was being punished without just cause left me feeling powerless and vulnerable. Tears became a constant companion as I grappled with the unfairness of it all.

During my time in custody, some of the athletes whom I had once mentored paid a visit, ostensibly under the guise of humanitarian concern. However, their true intention was to send a clear message of condemnation. Their presence served as a stark reminder of the isolation and betrayal I felt after the closure of the camp.

Being in police custody felt like an eternity, and for any reason, I couldn't imagine myself standing before the court for closing the camp

Despite my certainty of innocence and the roots of for my arrest, the prospect of facing prison time for a crime I didn't commit filled me with dread. I couldn't shake off the harrowing stories I had heard from inmates about life behind bars. The gruesome images of smuggling contraband, enduring dehumanizing treatments, and the general brutality of prison life flashed before my eyes.

Surrounded by hardened criminals during two days, I witnessed disturbing scenes of individuals resorting to desperate measures to cope with their confinement. Some concealed cigarettes in unimaginable places, others stashed money in forbidden crevices, and a few even ingested items to smuggle them into the prison.

Despite my past achievements as a runner, my current situation shocked those who recognized me, highlighting the abrupt and unjust nature of my downfall. Faced with the grim reality of imprisonment, I made a solemn decision that I would rather face death than endure the horrors of life behind bars for a crime I didn't commit.

In a last-ditch effort, I pleaded with the officer in charge who demanded bribery. I showed him invitation for Beijing marathon in China. This being the right information he was waiting he demanded me to part with Ksh. 80,000 to buy my freedom. I promised to give him on my return from Beijing marathon and he accepted.

***

For the next six months, my training was overshadowed by the looming specter of court appearances. Despite the hurdles, I was determined to participate in the Beijing Marathon once again later that year. However, a new obstacle emerged as I attempted to leave the country for the event.

I always packed my racing flats in advance and keep them in my house ready. On the day of my travel, I stopped briefly at home to picked up my racing shoes. At home I asked my wife to hand me the packed shoe pocket I had prepared. She secretly looked the shoe I had packed and didn't like it because it appeared used; according to her it did not sound ok to carry a used shoe while there are new shoe lying around. Un aware that the shoe was specific for competition, she decided exchanged the shoe with another new shoe and never informed me. I hurriedly and unaware took the bag pair of racing flat in a concealed bag and off I left for Beijing.

In China, I encountered yet more drama. Two days after arrival while in a hotel in Beijing, I noticed that I had the wrong racing flat. It was not broken into and was tight on me. I enquired how far it was to the nearest shoe store and if I could get ride to buy new flats. The elite coordinator told me he cannot help with anything in that nature and I should contact my manager. I was devastated; my only option was to remove inner soles cut holes around its edges to make it loose.

I looked around the hotel not even a nail cutter. At the hotel's small kiosk; nothing sharp enough I could use to poke holes on the shoe. I approached one hotel employee and asked him to provide me with a kitchen knife. It sounded weird and he told me it not possible because if anything happens like suicide or attack to someone the entire hotel will be in great danger.

 Luckily on Friday after my morning run I saw a tray delivered to my room. It was covered, Upon opening it was a huge cake, and next to the cake was a nice cake. The hotel had decided to serve special cakes to all international runners. Unknown to them, this was God send. Before even thinking about the cake, and with the words shared by the employee when I tried to borrow kitchen knife in mind, I had no time to waste just in case they might change their mind a retrieve the knifes from the cake. I poked the racing flat left right and middle. I tore every corner that would feel holding my blood flow. The shoe appeared to have been run over by a by a military tank but I was ready for the race.

One more challenge surfaced, I was denied any appearance fee, while inexperienced runners were generously compensated with fees ranging from three to eight thousand dollars. The Chinese elite coordinator explained that I was excluded from appearance fees because they didn't trust my fitness level. He told me that I was given a chance to prove myself on the field.

With no bargaining power, I was prepared for the race. On race day, we were transported to Tiananmen Square, the starting point for that year's events. As elite athletes, we were allocated a special bus parked among school buses. I left my racing gear and bag inside the bus where I had been seated.

After our warm-up, just moments before the race was set to begin, I realized my racing kit was missing; my shoes, vest, shorts, and even my running bib. Panic set in as I frantically searched, suspecting foul play from those who wished to sabotage my participation.

I immediately approached the race director, explaining my predicament. In a rare act of leniency, the race was halted for ten minutes to allow me to retrieve my gear if it could be found. Ironically, my kit had been surreptitiously stashed inside one of the yellow school buses. Within minutes of the announcement, students discovered it, and I hastily made my way to the starting line, grateful for the opportunity to compete despite the obstacles placed in my path.

The race consumed my focus from start to finish. I knew I was surrounded by vultures in running gears; therefore, I maintained vigilance over my surroundings, monitoring every step, every competitor ahead and behind me. In the initial kilometers, the pace fluctuated until it settled around three minutes per kilometer.

Around the 20-kilometer mark, the runner I suspected of sabotage surged ahead, opening up a ten-meter gap and quickening the pace to two minutes and 55 seconds per kilometer. For the next three kilometers, no one dared to challenge him, but we all maintained the same pace and kept a constant distance behind him.

At the 25-kilometer mark, his lead began to falter, and I seized the opportunity to take charge of the pack, now comprising seven athletes. During the competition my toes and heel started hurting terribly. As we reached the 35-kilometer mark I was experiencing excruciating pain; at the time I was 3rd while other runners were chasing me at close range. I had to decide between dropping out which at that distance wasn't logical or keep sustaining more injuries and finish top three. I remained at the helm, I lacked confident in my pace due to the pain in my feet. Every step landing on the ground felt as if extra blood was pumped in my toes and heels but I kept on. I knew I needed to break away from the pack, but I also needed to ensure I didn't overextend myself.

My perseverance drove me to a different level of performing while if pain.

Recalling my training in Embu, where I had practiced a ten-minute threshold on speed endurance, I felt assured. I decided to make my move; with two kilometers to go I sprinted out ahead. With a burst of energy, I surged forward, catching everyone off guard with a pace of 2.55 seconds per kilometer. I continued to accelerate all the way to the finish line, leaving the pack behind in my wake. With the same spirit, I won the race with great pain. From that day, I did not wear shoes for a week due to damaged toe nails.

***

Returning to Embu meant facing the conditions for money extorsion from the police; a payment of eighty thousand Kenyan shillings, equivalent to one thousand five hundred US dollars was expected to save me from humiliation. Reluctantly, I complied and the officer walked away with my hard-earned money.

After experiencing such disappointment and the subsequent realization of my limitations in effecting change as an individual, particularly in enlightening my community about unity, cohesion, and the benefits of transferring running skills to the next generation. I reached a pivotal moment. Circumstances, which I won't delve into here presented me with an opportunity to relocate to Canada.

Walking away, I carried the weight of regret for not being able to pass on my training secrets to the next generation. It pained me deeply to feel that I hadn't given the young athletes the best of what I had to offer. The pervasive greed and selfishness in our culture remained the greatest obstacle to the robust growth of running careers among our youth. I strongly believed that something needed to change, that the barriers within running administration needed to be addressed to prevent the talent from being wasted and lost in the depths of despair.

Through the hardships and challenges faced in the realm of running fraternity, I've learned invaluable lessons that extend far beyond the finish line. Each obstacle, setback, and adversity has been a crucible for personal growth and resilience. Despite the bureaucratic hurdles, financial constraints, and logistical nightmares, the unwavering spirit of camaraderie among athletes shines through. We've forged bonds of solidarity, finding strength in unity as we navigate the treacherous terrain of sports administration and competition.

At the heart of this journey lies the indomitable human spirit, fueled by a passion for running that transcends the limitations imposed by circumstance. Through perseverance and determination, we've confronted each obstacle head-on, refusing to be deterred by the myriad challenges that stand in our path. Our experiences have taught us the value of adaptability, resourcefulness, and community support, showing us that together, we are capable of overcoming even the most daunting of challenges. I learned that in Kenya one can be anointed for sainthood one day and crucified the next day.

As I reflect on my journey through the trials and tribulations of the running fraternity, I am reminded of the resilience of the human spirit and the enduring power of perseverance. Each step forward, no matter how arduous, brings us closer to our goals and reaffirms our commitment to the sport we love. Though the road ahead may be fraught with uncertainty, I am filled with a sense of optimism and determination, knowing that with unwavering resolve and the support of my fellow athletes, there is no obstacle too great to overcome.

Relocating to Canada came with its own set of challenges, but I was grateful for the welcoming gesture extended by the country. However, I soon realized that showcasing my full running potential would be hindered by certain policies that restrict certain functions for immigrants. As I awaited my chances to prove myself in Canada, I found that my age had unexpectedly become a limiting factor.

ENDS

www.ingramcontent.com/pod-product-compliance
Lightning Source LLC
Chambersburg PA
CBHW071216090426
42736CB00014B/2846